Waterstone's Guide to Poetry Books

Edited by Nick Rennison

Contents

Since the opening of our first branch in 1982 Waterstones has been committed to offering readers as wide a choice of poetry, both classic and contemporary, as possible. Today, in more than a hundred branches, we continue to believe in the excitement, insight and pleasure to be found in poetry and our shops provide a selection of books unmatched by any other high street bookseller for range and variety. This guide reflects that commitment to poetry and offers its own selection of the best and most interesting titles currently available by poets as diverse as Ben Jonson and Benjamin Zephaniah, Chaucer and Wendy Cope. We make no claims that the selection of books and poets in the guide is definitive or comprehensive. Poetry is too various and too protean to be contained by such a guide. However we are confident that the guide provides a generous introduction to the richness and diversity of poetry in English and that the imagination and intelligence of the reader will be engaged by the poets represented. In addition to brief commentaries on the poets, written by Waterstone's booksellers and poetry buyers, the guide also contains a number of previously unpublished poems by contemporary writers, including Simon Armitage, Don Paterson, Helen Dunmore, Thomas Lynch and C. K. Williams, and offers money off a wide range of titles from leading poetry publishers Faber & Faber and Carcanet and from the Everyman Pocket Poets Library.

Anglo-Saxon and Medieval Verse

Beowulf

The most famous and important of Old English poems, Beowulf was probably written in the 8th century, although its setting is Denmark two or three centuries earlier and the material it uses links it into a network of other legends of Germanic Europe in the period. The first half of the poem tells of the eponymous hero's battle against the monster Grendel and his even more monstrous mother. The second half takes place fifty years later as the ageing Beowulf is called to a final battle against a marauding dragon, a battle in which he is mortally wounded. The poem's emphasis on the feasting and fighting central to a warrior society and on the deeds of its hero is linked with a wider examination of the relationship of an individual to his society and of the nature of good and evil, together with an underlying moral thread which appears to demand a Christian interpretation.

Beowulf
Penguin pbk £5.99

Chaucer, Geoffrey
(C. 1343 -1400)

The first great poet in the language and, in Dryden's words, 'the father of English poetry'. His work shows the enormous influence of French and Italian verse and a good part of his genius lay in his ability to refashion continental models into a particularly English mould, thus developing the language as a literary medium. His most famous work, *The Canterbury Tales,* although unfinished, is an ironic survey of his society, from courtly knight to bawdy miller, in the form of tales told by specific characters in the course of a pilgrimage from Southwark to Canterbury. His longest complete poem *Troilus and Criseyde,* adapted from a work by Boccaccio, is a narrative of fated love set in the Trojan War.

The Canterbury Tales
(trans. Nevill Coghill)
Penguin pbk £3.99

The Canterbury Tales
(trans. David Wright)
Oxford UP pbk £3.95

The Riverside Chaucer
Oxford UP pbk £9.95

Troilus and Criseyde
(trans. Nevill Coghill)
Penguin pbk £3.95

Dunbar, William
(1456? - ?BEFORE 1530)

The little that is known of Dunbar's life indicates that he was in the service of the Scots king James IV and he certainly travelled abroad in France and England, probably on diplomatic missions for the king. Dunbar's achievements, in what was a period of great vigour in Scottish poetry, are substantial and cover a wide range of poetic forms and styles. *Lament for the Makaris* is

Illustration from *The Canterbury Tales*

an interesting reworking of familiar concerns about the transitoriness and mutability of life. *The Flyting of Dunbar and Kennedy*, in contrast, is an energetic exercise in invective in which the poet and an arch rival exchange linguistically inventive abuse in a ritual 'flyting'. He also wrote a number of short, religious poems and dream visions, such as *The Sevin Deidly Synnes* in which the poet witnesses a devil leading the souls of the dead in a macabre dance.

Selected Poems
Longman pbk £18.99

from The Canterbury Tales
by Geoffrey Chaucer

Whan that Aprill with his shoures soote

The droghte of March hath perced to the roote,

And bathed every veyne in swich licour

Of which vertu engendred is the flour;

Whan Zephirus eek with his sweete breeth

Inspired hath in every holt and heeth

The tendre croppes, and the yonge sonne

Hath in the Ram his halve cours yronne,

And smale foweles maken melodye,

That slepen al the nyght with open ye

(So priketh hem nature in hir corages);

Thanne longen folk to goon on pilgrimages,

And palmeres for to seken straunge strondes,

To ferne halwes, kowthe in sondry londes;

And specially from every shires ende

Of Engelond to Caunterbury they wende,

The hooly blisful martir for to seke,

That hem hath holpen whan that they were seeke.

Gawain Poet

The identity of the author of *Sir Gawain and the Green Knight* is unknown although most scholars agree that the same man is responsible for three other poems *(Pearl, Patience* and *Cleanness)* found in the one surviving manuscript. The poems were probably written about 1375 in a north west midlands dialect often very different from the language of Chaucer. *Sir Gawain and the Green Knight* is a 2,500 line alliterative poem set in the court of King Arthur and telling the story of one of the knights and the consequences of his acceptance of a challenge from a mysterious visitor to the court. The narrative skill and vivid language make this one of the greatest and most admired works in Middle English.

Sir Gawain and the Green Knight
(ed. John Burrow)
Penguin pbk £5.99

Sir Gawain and the Green Knight
(ed. Tolkien & Gordon)
Oxford UP pbk £9.99

Gower, John
(c. 1330 - 1408)

A friend of Chaucer and a man of wide learning Gower wrote with accomplishment in three languages - French, Latin and English. His principal work in English is *Confessio Amantis,* a collection of tales, some of them paralleling stories in the Canterbury Tales and other works by Chaucer, set in the framework of the confession of a lover, Amans, to a priest of Venus. In Gower's own words the tales are 'somwhat of lust, somwhat of love' and are told in the demanding metric form of octosyllabic couplets.

Selected Poetry
Carcanet pbk £6.95

Henryson, Robert
(c. 1424 - c. 1506)

Along with Dunbar, Henryson was the most prominent figure in the group of diverse Scottish poets known, slightly misleadingly, as the Scottish Chaucerians. Henryson does owe a debt to Chaucer, particularly in his major work, *The Testament of Cresseid,* a sympathetic but moralising sequel to Chaucer's *Troilus & Criseyde.* However he was much more than a mere imitator and his subtle reworking of the story is the achievement of a major poet.

Selected Poems
Carcanet pbk £5.95

Langland, William
(c. 1330 - c. 1386)

Very little is certainly known of the author of *Piers Plowman.* The younger (or possibly illegitimate) son of an Oxford gentleman, he was probably in minor orders. His masterpiece exists in three different versions and the assumption is that he worked on and revised the poem throughout the last twenty years of his life. The visions of the dreamer-narrator as he undertakes a pilgrimage in search of truth and the love of God form what has been described as 'the greatest Christian poem in our language', a poem filled with powerful imaginative passages and a rich use of humour and colloquialism.

Piers the Ploughman
Penguin pbk £4.99

Elizabethan and 17th Century Verse

Donne, John
(1572-1631)

The finest of the so-called 'Metaphysical Poets', Donne wrote poetry throughout his adult life but it was only collected and published after his death. During his lifetime he was renowned for the brilliant sermons he preached as Dean of St Paul's, a position he had attained after long years in obscurity following what was deemed an unsuitable marriage. The intellectual depth and allusiveness of his satires, elegies and love poetry have found particular favour with twentieth century poets such as T.S.Eliot who wrote approvingly 'a thought to Donne was an experience; it modified his sensibility'. Donne's capacity to create imaginative conceits which yoke together heterogeneous elements in his poetry often surprises the reader into new ways of responding to the language.

Complete English Poems
Penguin pbk £8.99

Complete English Poems
Dent pbk £6.99

Poetical Works
Oxford UP pbk £9.99

Selected Poems
Penguin pbk £4.99

Virtue
by George Herbert.

Sweet Day, so cool, so calm, so bright,

The bridal of the earth and sky :

The dew shall weep thy fall tonight,

       For thou must die.

Sweet rose, whose hue angry and brave

Bids the rash gazer wipe his eye :

Thy root is ever in its grave,

       And thou must die.

Sweet spring, full of sweet days and roses,

A box where sweets compacted lie

My music shows ye have your closes,

       And all must die.

Only a sweet and virtuous soul,

Like seasoned timber, never gives ;

But though the whole world turn to coal,

       Then chiefly lives.

Herbert, George
(1593-1633)

A member of an old and prominent family, Herbert renounced the worldly preferment open to him after he was elected to the prestigious position of public orator at Cambridge and chose instead the life of a country parson. He died shortly before his fortieth birthday, sending his poems to a friend with the instructions to publish them if he thought they might 'turn to the advantage of any dejected soul'. His poetry is often loosely described as 'metaphysical' and the ingenuity of his conceits does recall that of Donne. However, Herbert's quieter and more meditative voice is very different from the more flamboyant versification of the older poet.

Complete English Poems
Penguin pbk £8.99

Herrick, Robert
(1591-1674)

Herrick's long life was divided between London, where as a young man he was a leading member of the circle of poets who surrounded Ben Jonson, and Devon to which he was an initially reluctant exile as a parish priest but which he grew to love as the home of traditions and customs that the Puritans were attempting to suppress. His lyric poetry is rightly still admired and he is, in all his writings, a poet with an almost faultless ear for the sounds of verse.

Selected Poems
Carcanet pbk £5.95

Hymn to Diana
by Ben Jonson

Queen and huntress, chaste and fair,

Now the sun is laid to sleep,

Seated in thy silver chair,

State in wonted manner keep :

Hesperus entreats thy light,

Goddess excellently bright.

Earth, let not thy envious shade

Dare itself to interpose;

Cynthia's shining orb was made

Heaven to clear when day did close:

Bless us then with wishèd sight

Goddess excellently bright.

Lay thy bow of pearl apart

And thy crystal-shining quiver;

Give unto the flying hart

Space to breathe, how short soever:

Thou that mak'st a day of night-

Goddess excellently bright.

Howard, Henry
EARL OF SURREY (C. 1517 - 47)

Surrey's short life was ended when he was accused of treason on the accession of Edward VI and beheaded but he was largely responsible for two major innovations in English poetry. Like his near contemporary Wyatt, he studied the sonnet form used by Italian poets, particularly Petrarch, but his own sonnets were largely in the 'English' form later used by Shakespeare, a form which appears to have been Surrey's own invention. An even more influential innovation was his use of blank verse in his translation of two books of Virgil's Aeneid.

Selected Poems
Carcanet pbk £5.95

Jonson, Ben
(1572-1637)

Better known as a playwright, Jonson was also a considerable poet and, although he was not formally appointed as the first Poet Laureate, the pension granted to him in 1616 by James I essentially marked the inauguration of that position. His early life was turbulent and he narrowly escaped hanging in 1598 after killing an actor in a duel but he became the leading literary figure of the Jacobean period, the centre of a circle of writers who styled themselves 'the sons of Ben'. His poetry is at its best in his epigrams and in a handful of elegant lyrics based on classical models.

Complete Poems
Penguin pbk £11.00

Epigrams & The Forest
Carcanet pbk £6.95

Selected Works
Oxford UP pbk £11.95

Marlowe, Christopher
(1564-1593)

The stormy events of Marlowe's life and the mysterious circumstances surrounding his death in a tavern brawl are the stuff from which legends are created and the debate about how far and in what way he was involved in the murky underworld of Elizabethan espionage continues in recent works such as Charles Nicholl's much-praised *The Reckoning*. He was an admired and influential dramatist and it is hard to imagine how Shakespeare's early plays would have developed without the example of Marlowe. His non-dramatic verse includes the erotic narrative poem *Hero and Leander*, translations of the Latin poets Ovid and Lucan and a number of well-known lyrics.

Complete Poems and Plays
Dent pbk £6.99

Complete Poems and Translations
Penguin pbk £8.99

Marvell, Andrew
(1621 -1678)

Marvell, despite spending the years of the Civil War on the continent, was a committed supporter of Cromwell and was active politically in the period of the Commonwealth. Some of his finest verse was written on political subjects and he was also renowned in his lifetime as a satirist, attacking the financial and sexual corruption of the restored Stuart court with savage wit and irony. As a lyric poet he was virtually unknown in his life and neglected for two centuries until the enthusiasm of Grierson and Eliot rescued him from oblivion and raised him to his current status as the most popular of late metaphysical poets. His capacity to revitalise conventional poetic material with his oblique intelligence and his command of rhythm and phrasing is particularly rewarding for the modern reader.

Complete Poems
Penguin pbk £8.50

Selected Poems
Carcanet pbk £5.95

Eric Gill illustration for Shakespeare Sonnets

Milton, John
(1608-1674)

The weighty dignity and
sonorous diction of Milton's
verse is unique : he created a
style and language which
have haunted poets ever since
and have been a formative
influence on all subsequent
ventures into the epic form.
His work stretches from the
youthful poems written before
the Civil War - *Lycidas, Comus,
L'Allegro, Il Penseroso* - to the
great works in which he
wrestled with the relationship
of man to God and with the
wreck of his own political
beliefs brought about by
Charles II's restoration:
Paradise Lost, Paradise Regained
and *Samson Agonistes*.

Poetical Works
OUP pbk £10.99

Paradise Lost
Longman pbk £19.99

Paradise Lost
Penguin pbk £4.99

Raleigh, Sir Walter
(1552 - 1618)

Raleigh was a man who knew
the highs and lows of royal
favour and patronage. Under
Elizabeth I he was one of the
nation's leading explorers and
colonizers. Under James I he
was imprisoned in the Tower
for thirteen years on largely
trumped-up charges of treason
and only released to lead a
doomed expedition in search
of El Dorado, the failure of
which resulted in his execution.
His poetry is beset by uncertainties about authenticity but
those that are certainly ascribed
reveal an elegiac writer,
understandably interested in
the vagaries of fortune.

Selected Writings
Penguin pbk £5.99

Shakespeare, William
(1564-1616)

Shakespeare's principal non-
dramatic verse consists of 154
sonnets, first printed in 1609
but probably written in the
1590s, and the two narrative
poems *Venus and Adonis* and
The Rape of Lucrece. The sonnets
follow the course of the writer's
relationship with a young man
of high social position. Much
ink has been spilled in efforts
to identify the young man and
the other characters - the Dark
Lady and the rival poet - who
appear in the sequence but
viewing the sonnets as some
kind of hidden autobiography
can easily stand in the way of
appreciating Shakespeare's

skilful use and reworking of a
form and of themes common in
the period. The two narrative
poems are retellings of stories
from the classical past - the first
a version of the goddess Venus'
fated love for a mortal and the
second an adaptation of a semi-
legendary exemplum of female
virtue taken from Roman history.

The Narrative Poems
Penguin pbk £6.99

Sonnets
Penguin pbk £6.99

Sonnets
Oxford UP pbk £6.99

Sidney, Sir Philip
(1554-1586)

Sidney's reputation as the
perfect Renaissance soldier and
poet, man of letters and man
of action was sealed by his
death at the siege of Zutphen.
In some ways this heroic
reputation has outstripped the
documented achievements of
his life but the sonnet
sequence *Astrophel and Stella*,
addressed to Penelope
Devereux, is a striking exercise
in an exacting metrical form
and *A Defence of Poetry* is the
most substantial and influential
work of criticism in English
before Dryden.

Selected Poems
Oxford UP pbk £5.95

Selected Poems
Penguin pbk £6.99

Selected Writings
Carcanet pbk £6.95

Skelton, John
(c. 1460 - 1529)

Skelton was tutor to the young Henry VIII and enjoyed periodic favour at court despite inconveniently satirical opinions on politics and the Church. The idiosyncrasy of his favoured metre, a headlong, breathless doggerel with frequently recurring rhymes, has led to him being often dismissed - Pope referred to him as 'beastly Skelton' - but in the 20th century he has found admirers in Auden and Robert Graves amongst others.

Complete English Poems
Penguin pbk £11.00

Selected Poems
Carcanet pbk £5.95

Contemporary woodcut of Skelton

Spenser, Edmund
(1552 - 1599)

Spenser pursued an active political career in Elizabethan Ireland and was a friend of many of the leading figures of the period, including Sidney, Raleigh and the Earl of Essex. He published a number of volumes of poetry in his own lifetime but his contemporary fame rested, as does his posthumous reputation, on the huge allegory of *The Faerie Queene*. This work, unfinished in the form he originally intended it, nonetheless provided England with an epic chivalric romance to rival Tasso and Ariosto and had a crucial influence on future English poets from Milton to Keats and beyond. His pastoral works and the marriage poem *Epithalamion*, probably written to celebrate his own second marriage, have also been much admired.

Poetical Works
Oxford UP pbk £11.99

The Faerie Queene
Penguin pbk £16.00

Traherne, Thomas
(1637 -1674)

Traherne led a life of comparative obscurity and seclusion, publishing only one book of prose in his lifetime. The discovery of his verse and the *Centuries of Meditation,* a prose work which includes probably the first convincing description of childhood experience in English literature, indicates how serendipitous the survival of an important poet can be. For more than two centuries the manuscripts passed through unknown hands until they were picked off a London bookstall in 1896 and identified as the work of Traherne. Traherne's mysticism, his rapturous joy in creation and his belief in the need for the adult to recover the primal vision of the child are unmatched in his period.

Selected Poems and Prose
Penguin pbk £9.99

Selected Writings
Carcanet pbk £4.95

Vaughan, Henry
(1621 - 1695)

Born in Breconshire, the son of a Welsh gentleman, Vaughan led an unsettled life in the years of the Civil War before practising medicine in his native county. His twin brother Thomas was the author of many treatises on alchemy and mysticism and Vaughan himself, after publishing several volumes of secular poetry, began to produce the great religious poetry of his maturity, which clearly demonstrates the influence of the tradition in which his brother was working. Vaughan's interest in the bonds between microcosm and macrocosm and in the working of God's purpose through the natural world are distinctively embodied in the best of his verse.

Complete Poems
Penguin pbk £9.99

Selected Poems
Carcanet pbk £5.95

Wyatt, Sir Thomas
(1503 -1542)

Wyatt's career as a diplomat in the service of Henry VIII was the means by which he was introduced to the Italian poets, especially Petrarch, whose sonnets he translated and imitated. His unfortunate involvement with Anne Boleyn, possibly as one of her lovers, very nearly cost him his life but he emerged from a period in the Tower to resume his career. His prosodic irregularity, especially when contrasted with Surrey's smoothness, has often met with criticism (and indeed editorial correction) but others have admired the complexity and originality of his love poems.

Complete Poems
Penguin pbk £11.00

Selected Poems
Carcanet pbk £6.95

Remembrance
by Sir Thomas Wyatt

They flee from me, that sometime did me seek
With naked foot, stalking in my chamber.
I have seen them gentle, tame, and meek,
That now are wild, and do not remember
That sometime they put themselves in danger
To take bread at my hand; and now they range
Busily seeking with a continual change.

Thanked be fortune it hath been otherwise
Twenty times better; but once, in special,
In thin array, after a pleasant guise,
When her loose gown from her shoulders did fall,
And she me caught in her arms long and small,
Therewith all sweetly did me kiss
And softly said, 'Dear heart, how like you this?'

It was no dream; I lay broad waking:
But all is turned, thorough my gentleness,
Into a strange fashion of forsaking;
And I have leave to go of her goodness,
And she also to use newfangleness.
But since that I so kindly am served,
I would fain know what she hath deserved.

Restoration and 18th Century Verse

Chatterton, Thomas
(1752 - 1770)

The powerful effect on the Romantic imagination of Chatterton's short life and despairing death at his own hand has overshadowed his work. 'The marvellous boy', as Wordsworth described him, is seldom read but the pseudo-archaic poems which he wrote and passed off as the writings of a non-existent medieval monk occasionally transcend pastiche and attain a lyric excellence of their own.

Selected Poems
Carcanet pbk £5.95

Collins, William
(1721 - 1759)

In the course of a troubled life - his last years were plagued by bouts of severe melancholia - Collins wrote relatively little but his *Odes on Several Descriptive and Allegoric Subjects* proved to have a lasting influence on poetry in the 18th century. Later poets responded strongly to the 'sublimity and splendour' which, Dr Johnson noted, were characteristic of his best writing.

Poems of Gray, Collins and Goldsmith
Longman pbk £25.00

Cowper, William
(1731 - 1800)

Evangelical religion was both the blessing and the bane of Cowper's life. The only ease and security he knew came from his faith, and from the friends with whom he shared it, but he was also driven to acute suffering by those periods of paranoid delusion in which he was convinced of his own unforgivable sinfulness and the imminence of eternal damnation. It is an irony that he is best known for one of the great comic poems of the language - *The Diverting History of John Gilpin*.
His versatility as a poet was considerable and his other works include satires, evangelical hymns, lines on the natural world which point forward to the concerns of the Romantics and a long celebration of country life, *The Task*.

Selected Poems
Carcanet pbk £5.95

Crabbe, George
(1754 - 1832)

Crabbe was born in Suffolk and practised briefly there as a doctor before travelling to London in an attempt to establish a literary career. After early setbacks he was introduced to Burke who encouraged his ambitions and introduced him to influential friends. The result was *The Village*, an unsentimental work contrasting the grim realities of rural life with the pastoral fantasies of poets. Much of the rest of Crabbe's life was spent as a rural churchman and, after a long period during which he published nothing, the last twenty years of his life saw the publication of a series of varied stories in verse (*The Borough* includes Peter Grimes, the source for Britten's opera) which give precise and closely observed portraits of village life and landscape.

Selected Poems
Penguin pbk £7.99

Selected Poetry
Carcanet pbk £6.95

The Poplar-Field
by William Cowper

The poplars are felled, farewell to the shade
And the whispering sound of the cool colonnade,
The winds play no longer, and sing in the leaves,
Nor Ouse on his bosom their image receives.

Twelve years have elapsed since I last took a view
Of my favourite field and the bank where they grew,
And now in the grass behold they are laid,
And the tree is my seat that once lent me a shade.

The blackbird has fled to another retreat
Where the hazels afford him a screen from the heat,
And the scene where his melody charmed me before,
Resounds with his sweet-flowing ditty no more.

My fugitive years are all hasting away,
And I must ere long lie as lowly as they,
With a turf on my breast, and a stone at my head,
Ere another such grove shall arise in its stead.

'Tis a sight to engage me, if any thing can,
To muse on the perishing pleasures of man;
Though his life be a dream, his enjoyments, I see,
Have a being less durable even than he.

Dryden, John
(1631 - 1700)

Most of Dryden's early writings were for the theatre, although he published poems that celebrated the restoration of the monarchy and *Annus Mirabilis*, a poem in quatrains about the Anglo-Dutch War and the Great Fire. He was made Poet Laureate in 1668. The troubled constitutional and religious politics of Charles II's reign prompted Dryden to produce the great satires *MacFlecknoe* and *Absalom and Achitophel* in which he used the biblical story to make parallels with Monmouth's claims to the succession to Charles. In later life he became a Catholic which lost him his court positions and many of his later works were in the politically less compromising field of translation. His versions of Vergil are particularly fine. Dryden is one of the greatest of English poets and a major figure in the history of criticism. His wit and his enormous technical skill enabled him to perfect the heroic couplet, the favoured metrical form for poets throughout the following century, a century in which his influence continued to be strongly felt.

Poems and Prose
Penguin pbk £6.99

Dryden
(Oxford Authors)
Oxford UP pbk £12.99

Portrait of John Dryden

Gay, John
(1685 - 1732)

Many of Gay's best ballads appear in his most enduring work *The Beggar's Opera* and its sequel but he was a versatile writer in a number of styles and a friend of all the major figures of his period, including Pope and Swift. *Trivia* (sub-titled The Art of Walking the Streets of London) is a lively work and a mine of information about everyday life in the Georgian capital.

Selected Poems
Carcanet pbk £5.95

Goldsmith, Oliver
(1730 - 1774)

Dramatist, novelist, poet, hack journalist, Goldsmith was a man whose hopeless improvidence meant he was always on the brink of ruin and he was frequently obliged to write his way out of financial disaster. His novel *The Vicar of Wakefield* and the comedy *She Stoops to Conquer* are his best known works but he wrote a good deal of light verse and, most importantly, *The Deserted Village,* a nostalgic evocation of rural life before the incursion of trade and the mercantile spirit.

Selected Writings
Carcanet pbk £6.95

**Poems of Gray,
Collins and Goldsmith**
Longman pbk £25.00

Gray, Thomas
(1716 - 1771)

Few lives could be quieter or less eventful than that of Gray who, apart from two years travelling on the continent, spent most of his time at Cambridge, absorbed in antiquarian and historical studies. His *Elegy Written in a Country Churchyard* was originally published anonymously but its fame grew so rapidly that its authorship was soon known and indeed Gray was later offered the Poet Laureateship, which he declined. The poem is one of the best known in the language and studded with familiar quotations. Gray's other poems show his interest in the Sublime, that characteristic notion of the second half of the eighteenth century, and in the picturesque and mark him as one of the pivotal writers in the movement away from neo-classical lucidity towards the development of Romanticism.

**Poems of Gray,
Collins and Goldsmith**
Longman pbk £25.00

Selected Poems
Carcanet pbk £5.95

Johnson, Samuel
(1709 - 1784)

The subject of the most celebrated biography in the English language, Johnson spent his early career as an impoverished schoolmaster in the Midlands before moving to London in 1737 to pursue an equally impoverished life as a hack, Grub Street writer. The publication of his dictionary, in 1755, established his reputation and the grant of a state pension seven years later finally eased his financial anxieties. The period largely covered by Boswell's biography is the period of Johnson's pre-eminence in literary London and of his time as the moral and critical arbiter of his age. Johnson wrote poetry throughout his literary career but the two satires in imitation of Juvenal, *London* and *The Vanity of Human Wishes,* represent probably his most accomplished work.

Complete English Poems
Penguin pbk £7.99

Samuel Johnson
(Oxford Authors)
Oxford UP pbk £11.99

Pope, Alexander
(1688 - 1744)

Pope was the major poet of the Augustan period. His superb mastery of technique enabled him to achieve an exceptional rhythmic variety within the apparent restrictions of the heroic couplet, his most favoured metrical form. The wit of the early *Essay on Criticism* and the mock heroic *The Rape of the Lock* culminate in the swingeing satire of his burlesque epic *The Dunciad.* He spent long years and much energy on his translations of the Iliad and the Odyssey and his *Essay on Man* was intended to embody his views of the relations between man, nature and society.

Selected Poems of Alexander Pope
Penguin pbk £4.95

Poetical Works
OUP pbk £6.95

Smart, Christopher
(1722 - 1771)

Much of Smart's life was clouded by insanity - his madness took the form of a compulsion to public prayer which occasioned Dr. Johnson's tolerant remark, 'I'd as lief pray with Kit Smart as anyone else' - and he spent much time in an asylum in Bethnal Green. His most extraordinary work, *Jubilate Agno,* was composed in the asylum and remained unpublished until the 1930s. Its parallel sets of verses, based on the antiphonal principles of Hebrew poetry, are unique in English poetry. *A Song of David,* the most considerable of the poems published in his lifetime, contains 86 intricately arranged stanzas in celebration of the Creation and the Incarnation.

Religious Poetry
Carcanet pbk £5.95

Swift, Jonathan
(1667 - 1745)

Born in Dublin to English parents, Swift was a cousin of Dryden (who, legend has it, dismissed one of his earliest literary efforts with the words, 'Cousin Swift, you will never be a poet') and his life was largely divided between London and Dublin, between the acrimonious politics of the day and the affairs of the Anglican church in Ireland. He was for many years Dean of St Patrick's, Dublin and a prolific author of political pamphlets, satires and occasional verses. Most of these appeared anonymously and the only work for which he was paid was the one which posterity has most admired, if only as a tale for children, *Gulliver's Travels*. Swift's verse, like his prose, is marked by its simplicity and directness.

Complete Poems
Penguin pbk £16.00

Selected Poems
Carcanet pbk £5.95

Selected Poems
Penguin pbk £5.99

A Description of the Morning
by Jonathan Swift

Now hardly here and there an hackney-coach

Appearing, showed the ruddy morn's approach.

Now Betty from her master's bed had flown,

And softly stole to discompose her own.

The slipshod prentice from his master's door

Had pared the dirt, and sprinkled round the floor.

Now Moll had whirled her mop with dext'rous airs

Prepared to scrub the entry and the stairs.

The youth with broomy stumps began to trace

The kennel-edge, where wheels had worn the place.

The small-coal man was heard with cadence deep,

Till drowned in shriller notes of chimney-sweep.

Duns at his lordship's gate began to meet,

And Brickdust Moll had screamed through half a street.

The turnkey now his flock returning sees,

Duly let out a-nights to steal for fees.

The watchful bailiffs take their silent stands,

And schoolboys lag with satchels in their hands.

Thomson, James
(1700 - 1748)
In his lifetime, and for more than a century afterwards, Thomson was one of the most renowned of British poets (he was actually born in the Scottish Borders) and his best work, *The Seasons*, one of the most popular and most frequently reprinted of poems. Today his best known work - and few would be able to attach his name to it - is *Rule Britannia*, the verses for which he wrote to include in a stage masque. *The Seasons* is a landmark in poetic description of the natural world and was a large influence on later poets, particularly Wordsworth.

**The Seasons
& The Castle of Indolence**
Oxford UP pbk £11.99

Wilmot, John
EARL OF ROCHESTER
(1647 - 1680)

The most gifted of the 'Court Wits' who surrounded Charles II, Rochester was notorious for his womanising and drinking and for having, in Dr Johnson's imposing words, 'blazed out his youth and health in lavish voluptuousness'. This persona masked a complex and equivocal individual who wrote more frankly about sex than anyone in English before this century and is responsible for a series of exceptionally witty and emotionally challenging love lyrics. The rediscovery and reassessment of his work in the last twenty years was long overdue.

Complete Works
Penguin pbk £9.99

Debt to Pleasure
Carcanet pbk £6.95

Young, Edward
(1683 - 1765)

Young is another poet, like James Thomson, who enjoyed enormous fame in his own lifetime but has since fallen into obscurity. His best known work, *Night Thoughts,* `is, together with Gray's Elegy, the most noted example of the so-called 'graveyard' genre of verse, melancholy, reflective verses on mortality, which were extremely popular in the period.

Selected Poetry
Carcanet pbk £8.95

Love and Life
by John Wilmot, Earl of Rochester

All my past life is mine no more;
The flying hours are gone,
Like transitory dreams given o'er
Whose images are kept in store
By memory alone.

Whatever is to come is not:
How can it then be mine?
The present moment's all my lot,
And that, as fast as it is got,
Phyllis, is wholly thine.

Then talk not of inconstancy,
False hearts, and broken vows;
If I, by miracle, can be
This livelong minute true to thee,
'Tis all that heaven allows.

Romantic Verse

Blake's illustration of "Fire"
from *The Book of Urizen*

Blake, William
(1757 - 1827)

Blake received little formal education, although he studied at the Royal Academy of Art as a young man, and he passed his life in relative obscurity as an engraver in London. However throughout the time he was working for the London booksellers and for a number of varyingly helpful patrons he was also writing his own verses and elaborating his extraordinarily distinctive personal mythology. 'I must Create a System, or be enslav'd by another man's', he wrote and the mystical visions of the Prophetic books in which long flowing lines of verse alternate with phrases of terse and aphoristic clarity are the result of this self-imposed task. Blake was also a master of the lyric form as is clearly demonstrated by the *Songs of Innocence* and the *Songs of Experience*, which include 'Tyger! Tyger! burning bright' and others of his more accessible pieces. Received wisdom in his lifetime and later was that Blake was gifted but insane. Renewed interest in him this century has revealed a man who was not only a visionary but also a writer of witty epigrams, a critic of originality and a man who found his own method of investing the material and the mundane with the spiritual and transcendent.

Complete Poems
Penguin pbk £14.00

Songs of Innocence and Experience
Oxford UP pbk £7.99

Marriage of Heaven and Hell
Oxford UP pbk £7.99

William Blake
(Oxford Authors)
Oxford UP pbk £11.95

John Anderson my Jo
by Robert Burns

John Anderson my jo, John,
When we were first acquent
Your locks were like the raven,
Your bonnie brow was brent;
But now your brow is beld, John,
Your locks are like the snow;
But blessings on your frosty pow,
John Anderson, my jo.

John Anderson my jo, John,
We clamb the hill thegither;
And mony a canty day, John
We've had wi' ane anither:
Now we maun totter down, John,
And hand in hand we'll go;
And sleep thegither at the foot,
John Anderson my jo.

Burns, Robert
(1759 - 1796)

It is unfortunate that Burns' poetry has been overtaken by the legend of the 'heaven-taught ploughman', the miraculous and earthy man of the people who is celebrated every Burns Night. His poetry is far more interesting than the cultural stereotype suggests. His range and versatility, from satire to love lyrics and epigrams, his strong radical sympathies in an age of revolution, his sophisticated development of a composite, poetic Scots from a variety of dialects are all indicative of a poet in full command of his talents rather than some primitive genius dependent on the arbitrary visitations of the muse. His great love songs ('A Red, Red Rose' and 'O, Wert Thou in the Cauld Blast') indicate that the successful achievement of simple effects in verse demands the greatest technical skill.

Choice of Burns' Poems and Songs
Faber pbk £7.99

Poems and Songs
Oxford UP pbk £11.99

Byron, Lord George
(1788-1824)

In the broad context of European culture the persona Byron created for himself was as important as his poetry. The passionate and tormented 'Byronic hero' was the epitome of early 19th century Romanticism and his influence is strong in writers as diverse as Pushkin, Stendhal and the Brontë sisters. With the hindsight of more than 150 years it can be seen that the best qualities of his verse were the wit and mock-heroic inventiveness of *Don Juan* and that, in some ways, he was as much the last of the Augustans as the embodiment of Romanticism- it is no surprise that his own favourite poet was Pope.

Don Juan
Penguin pbk £14.00

Poetical Works
Oxford UP pbk £11.99

Selected Poems
Penguin pbk £7.99

Byron, The Saylor; after G. Sanders,1807

Clare, John
(1793 - 1864)

Born in Northamptonshire, the son of a labourer, Clare remained deeply attached to the place of his birth and his move away from it, together with the memories of the troubling loss of his first love, were probably the chief causes of the mental disturbance which led to his spending the last twenty years of his life in an asylum. He published several volumes of verse before his illness and continued to write throughout his incarceration. After a period of neglect Clare has found many champions in this century (including Edmund Blunden and C. Day-Lewis) and his best poems, complex evocations of landscape and loss can be read as simultaneous laments for his own expulsion from Eden and for the degeneration of rural England.

The Parish
Penguin pbk £4.99

Selected Poetry
Penguin pbk £6.99

The Shepherd's Calendar
Oxford UP pbk £6.99

Coleridge, S. Taylor

(1772 - 1834)

Samuel Taylor Coleridge by
P. Vandyke (1795)

The son of a Devon clergyman, Coleridge showed precocious talent as a schoolboy and, as an undergraduate, the instability that was to overshadow his life, disappearing for several months from Cambridge in order to enlist in the Dragoons under the unlikely pseudonym of Silas Tomkyn Comberbache. It was also at Cambridge that he first took opium which later came to dominate his life. Coleridge's friendship with Wordsworth, whom he met in 1797, was the central creative partnership of English Romanticism and the period when they lived and worked intimately together produced most of Coleridge's finest verse - *Christabel, Frost at Midnight, Kubla Khan* and *The Rime of the Ancient Mariner. Lyrical Ballads,* the selection of work by the two poets published in 1798, is a collection that marks a turning point in literary taste and sensibility. The next two decades were a time of escalating personal and creative difficulty for Coleridge as his addiction to opium grew, his marriage was destroyed by his obsessive love for Wordsworth's sister-in-law and his friendship with Wordsworth and others came under increasing strain. It is unsurprising that his only major poem of this period is called *Dejection: An Ode.* Only after a profound spiritual and physical crisis in 1814 was Coleridge able to emerge from the nearly suicidal depression into which he had plunged. In his later years, settled in a friend's house and weaned from his dependence on opium, he became a semi-legendary figure, the 'Sage of Highgate' as Carlyle called him, and an inspiration to the younger generation of Romantics. Although he wrote little poetry in his later years.

I am

by John Clare

I am: yet what I am none cares or knows,

My friends forsake me like a memory lost;

I am the self-consumer of my woes,

They rise and vanish in oblivious host,

Like shades in love and death's oblivion lost;

And yet I am, and live with shadows tost

Into the nothingness of scorn and noise,

Into the living sea of waking dreams,

Where there is neither sense of life nor joys

But the vast shipwreck of my life's esteems;

And e'en the dearest - that I loved the best -

Are strange - nay, rather stranger than the rest.

I long for scenes where man has never trod,

A place where woman never smiled or wept;

There to abide with my Creator, God,

And sleep as I in childhood sweetly slept:

Untroubling and untroubled where I lie,

The grass below - above the vaulted sky.

Coleridge's role as one of the two chief progenitors of English Romanticism was secure and his voluminous philosophical and critical writings grew in appreciation and influence.

Selected Poems
Penguin pbk £5.99

Selected Poetry
Carcanet pbk £7.95

Samuel Taylor Coleridge
(Oxford Authors)
Oxford UP £11.95

Keats, John
(1795 - 1821)

Apprenticed to an apothecary after leaving school, Keats was himself licensed to practise in the profession in 1816 but, despite financial insecurity,

abandoned it to concentrate on his poetry. His first book of verse was published in 1817 and, although it attracted some favourable attention, it was also one of the targets of a vicious critical assault from Blackwood's magazine on the alleged literary and social pretensions of what the magazine called the 'Cockney School' of poetry. Keats' younger brother died of tuberculosis the following year and Keats himself began to show symptoms of the same disease. Despite this he entered upon an extraordinary period of creativity, beginning his epic fragment *Hyperion,* writing *The Eve of St Agnes* and *La Belle Dame Sans Merci* and producing the great odes by which he is best remembered. His love affair with Fanny Brawne was conducted under the shadow of increasing ill health and, after a last journey to Italy in search of a climate more suited to his illness, he died in Rome in 1821. Keats' reputation grew in the decades following his death - Tennyson considered him the greatest poet of the century - and he still remains one of the principal figures in English Romanticism.

Complete Poems
Penguin pbk £9.99

Selected Poetry
Penguin pbk £4.99

Poetical Works
Oxford UP pbk £9.99

John Keats by C.A. Brown (1819)

**Lines written on a blank page
in a volume of Shakespeare's Poems**
by John Keats

Bright star, would I were steadfast as thou art -

Not in lone splendour hung aloft the night

And watching, with eternal lids apart,

Like Nature's patient, sleepless Eremite,

The moving waters at their priest-like task

Of pure ablution round earth's human shores,

Or gazing on the new soft-fallen mask

Of snow upon the mountains and the moors-

No - yet still steadfast, still unchangeable,

Pillowed upon my fair love's ripening breast,

To feel for ever its soft fall and swell,

Awake for ever in a sweet unrest,

Still, still to hear her tender-taken breath,

And so live ever - or else swoon to death.

Scott, Sir Walter
(1771 - 1832)

Scott is, of course, best remembered for the many widely read and enormously influential novels he wrote in the second half of his astonishingly productive career. However, he began his career as an editor and poet, producing volumes of old and contemporary ballads and a sequence of long poems based on his extensive knowledge of history, folklore and the narratives and chronicles of the Scottish borders. The best known of these is *Marmion*, a story set at the time of the battle of Flodden, but, despite the wide readership he gained in his lifetime for his verse narratives , he is now best remembered and read for the songs and lyrics which are scattered throughout them and throughout the later novels.

Selected Poems
Carcanet pbk £8.95

Shelley, Percy Bysshe
(1792 - 1822)

Although born into the heart of the ruling classes and educated at Eton and Oxford, Shelley was, from his teenage years, an extreme radical in politics and religion. He was finally expelled from Oxford after circulating a pamphlet he had written called *The Necessity of Atheism* and, quarrelling violently with his MP father, eloped to Scotland with his sixteeen year-old mistress. Together they spent a nomadic three years during which Shelley distributed his own pamphlets inveighing against his particular dislikes - royalty, meat-eating and religion were among them - and attempted to establish radical communes of like-minded individuals. He also wrote and published *Queen Mab*, his first great poem and

England in 1819
by Percy Bysshe Shelley

An old, mad,blind, despised, and dying king,-

Princes, the dregs of their dull race, who flow

Through public scorn, - mud from a muddy spring,-

Rulers who neither see, nor feel, nor know,

But leech-like to their fainting country cling,

Till they drop, blind in blood, without a blow, -

A people starved and stabbed in the untilled field,-

An army, which liberticide and prey

Makes as a two-edged sword to all who wield,-

Golden and sanguine laws which tempt and slay;

Religion Christless, Godless - a book sealed;

A Senate, - Time's worst statute unrepealed,-

Are graves from which a glorious Phantom may

Burst, to illumine our tempestuous day.

a visionary assault upon many of the same targets he had lined up in the pamphlets. Shelley's domestic arrangements, always complicated, became more complicated still when he eloped once again, this time with Mary Godwin, soon to be the author of *Frankenstein,* and her fifteen year-old step sister. After a further period of nomadic wanderings on the continent and in the British Isles, Shelley and his entourage settled in Italy where he produced a varied burst of major poetry, including the lyrical drama *Prometheus Unbound, The Mask of Anarchy,* perhaps the finest poem of political radicalism in the language, and *Ode to the West Wind.* The death of Keats in 1821 produced *Adonais,* an elegy in 55 Spenserian stanzas, and his platonic love affair with a local heiress resulted, not in another elopement, but in the autobiographical poem *Epipsychidion.* Shelley died in a boating accident, aged not yet thirty, and his romantic life and death have sometimes obscured his poetry. Yet his intellectual energy and originality are harnessed to an impressive command of poetic form and metre and he is undoubtedly one of the major figures of his time.

Poetical Works
Oxford UP pbk £11.99

Selected Poems
Dent pbk £6.95

Selected Poetry
Penguin pbk £5.99

Wordsworth, William
(1770 - 1850)

In the course of his long life, Wordsworth was deemed both hero and villain, often by the same judge - Byron wrote of him in a letter, 'Stupendous genius! damned fool' - and the trajectory of his career, from youthful radicalism to patriotic conservatism, is a familiar one. As a young man he was fired by the ideals of the French Revolution ('Bliss was it in that dawn to be alive/But to be young was very heaven') but he was rapidly disillusioned and he ended his life as Poet Laureate and eminent Victorian. The last years of the eighteenth century produced his intense creative collaboration with Coleridge. *Lyrical Ballads* was first published in 1798 and the second edition, with a provocative preface on poetic diction, was a call to poets to use 'the language really used by men' in their work. Soon after this Wordsworth moved to the Lake District where he was to live for the rest of his life and where he was to produce the great work of his middle years, the *Poems in Two Volumes* which include most of his finest lyrics, *The Excursion,* a poem in nine books which was originally planned as part of an even larger work and several other volumes which gradually increased his popularity with the reading public. His greatest work, *The Prelude,* remained unpublished at his death, although he had finished a complete version as early as 1805. He remodelled and reworked it several times and the final version was published posthumously in 1850.

Poetical Works
Oxford UP pbk £9.99

Poems Vol 1
Penguin pbk £16.00

Poems Vol 2
Penguin pbk £16.00

The Prelude
Penguin pbk £9.99

Selected Poems
Penguin pbk £7.99

Selected Poems
Dent pbk £6.99

Victorian Verse

Arnold, Matthew
(1822 - 1888)

The son of the great reforming headmaster of Rugby, Thomas Arnold, Matthew Arnold was born in the heart of the Victorian intellectual elite which he later criticised so strongly in such works as *Culture and Anarchy*. He spent his career as an inspector of schools and wrote and lectured widely on educational and social issues. He wrote and published poetry throughout his adult life but much of his best work dates from the 1850s when he produced *Empedocles on Etna* and a volume that included *The Scholar Gypsy* and *Sohrab and Rustum*, a narrative poem taken from a Persian epic. Perhaps his most famous poem *Dover Beach* embodies many of the most pressing anxieties of Victorian society, a society in which the old certitudes were being swiftly eroded.

Selected Poems
Penguin pbk £6.99

Selected Poems and Prose
Dent pbk £4.99

Selected Poetry
Carcanet pbk £7.95

Matthew Arnold
(Oxford Authors)
Oxford UP pbk £11.95

Barnes, William
(1801 - 1886)

Barnes is the most considerable writer of dialect verse in the language. His mastery of form and technique and his philological erudition and inventiveness are such that his poetry written in the Dorset dialect rises above the quaint provincialism to which such verse is usually condemned. He was greatly admired as a lyric poet by both Tennyson and Hardy and his use of language often prefigures the work of Hopkins, another admirer.

Selected Poems
Carcanet pbk £6.95

Destiny
by Matthew Arnold

Why each is striving, from of old,

To love more deeply than he can?

Still would be true, yet still grows cold?

- Ask of the powers that sport with man!

They yoked in him, for endless strife,

A heart of ice, a soul of fire;

And hurled him on the field of Life,

An aimless unallayed Desire.

Bronte, Emily
(1818 - 1848)

All three of the Brontë sisters (Charlotte, Emily and Anne) wrote poetry and their first published work was the pseudonymous *Poems of Currer, Ellis and Acton Bell*. Of the three, Emily was by far the most gifted and original poet. Her poetry reflects some of the same visionary mysticism and the sense of poorly suppressed violence which inform *Wuthering Heights*, published in 1847, the year before her death from consumption. In her biographical notice of her sister, published after Emily's death, Charlotte commented on the 'horror of great darkness' that seemed to brood over the novel and the same balefulness marks out much of her best poetry.

Complete Poems
Penguin pbk £6.99

Selected Poems of the Bronte Sisters
Carcanet pbk £5.95

Browning, Elizabeth Barrett
(1806 - 1861)

The eldest daughter of an autocratic owner of West Indian plantations, Elizabeth Barrett Browning's early adult life was shaped by two events - the illness which resulted in her invalidism and the death by drowning of her brother Edward which caused her lifelong grief. Her correspondence with and engagement to Robert Browning were kept a secret from her tyrannical father and the couple were obliged to elope to Italy where she spent the rest of her life, becoming a fierce partisan of Italian unity. Throughout her married life her poetic reputation stood higher than that of her husband and indeed her name was widely canvassed as Wordsworth's most appropriate successor as Poet Laureate when he died in 1850. Her magnum opus is the novel in verse *Aurora Leigh*, the life story of a woman writer, which has received much critical attention in recent years because of its feminist concerns and its speculations about the roles and responsibilities of women in society.

Aurora Leigh and Other Poems
Penguin pbk £5.99

Selected Poems
Carcanet pbk £5.95

Browning, Robert
(1812 - 1889)

Unconventionally educated at home, Browning was a man of wide and eclectic erudition who was frequently damned by the critics for the obscurity and impenetrability of his verse. *Sordello*, published in 1840, is now recognised as one of the finest long poems of the century but its poor reception by public and critics alike on publication caused severe and prolonged damage to Browning's reputation. He produced a series of plays and collections of shorter dramatic poems throughout the 1840s and, although attempts to stage some of the plays were disastrous, some of the poems (*My Last Duchess, The Pied Piper of Hamelin*) remain amongst his best known works. His elopement with and marriage to Elizabeth Barrett took him to Italy where he lived until the death of his wife in 1861. During this period he wrote the poems and dramatic monologues collected in *Men and Women* which went some way to re-establishing his name although he had to wait until after his wife's death and his return to England before he gained anything like the success to which his great rival and contemporary Tennyson was accustomed. Only with *The Ring and the Book*, a huge poem in blank verse about a lurid murder in 17th century Rome, published in monthly instalments in 1868-9, did he gain great popular acclaim. Browning was a master of the dramatic monologue and the intricate ironies he used in this form, together with his interest in grotesque subjects and his ability to alternate passages of great beauty with broken rhythms, discordances and colloquialisms ensured his continued interest to the generation of Pound and Eliot when many of his contemporaries seemed hopelessly outmoded.

Poems Vol 1
Penguin pbk £17.00

Poems Vol 2
Penguin pbk £15.00

Selected Poems
Penguin pbk £5.99

The Ring and the Book
Penguin pbk £15.00

Clough, Arthur Hugh
(1819 - 1861)

Clough is an interesting but neglected poet, embodying many of the doubts and anxieties which assailed the Victorian intellectual. Educated amidst the bracing certainties of Thomas Arnold's Rugby, he was thrown into tormenting religious misgivings when he arrived at Oxford and these remained with him throughout his life. He is remembered for some of his shorter poems, including the satirical take on the Ten Commandments *The New Decalogue,* and for two 'novels in verse', *The Bothie of Tober-na-Vuolich*, which tells the story of a student reading party in Scotland, and *Amours de Voyage,* about sensitive English travellers in Rome. After his early death he was commemorated in his friend Matthew Arnold's elegy *Thyrsis*.

Selected Poems
Carcanet pbk £6.95

Selected Poems
Penguin pbk £7.99

Hopkins, Gerard Manley
(1844 - 1889)

At school and at Oxford Hopkins showed enormous academic and artistic promise, made many friends, including Robert Bridges, later to be Poet Laureate, and wrote much poetry. After his conversion to Roman Catholicism he renounced most of this life and resolved to join the Jesuit movement, studying as a novice at Roehampton and Stonyhurst. As a Jesuit, Hopkins was directed to a varied number of posts, including exhausting spells in a number of industrial parishes, before being appointed Professor of Greek and Latin at University College, Dublin where he died of typhoid in 1889. Hopkins' poetic ambitions had been rekindled in 1876 when, with the encourage-ment of his rector, he wrote *The Wreck of the Deutschland* and, although this was rejected by a Jesuit magazine as too difficult for its readers, he continued to write poetry for the rest of his life. None of this poetry was published in his lifetime and Bridges, to whom Hopkins' literary remains were entrusted, felt unable to publish it until 1918, adjudging the public unready for Hopkins'

Meredith, George
(1828 - 1909)

Meredith was one of the most revered literary figures of the late Victorian and Edwardian eras but his star has waned in the time since his death and his novels, though several are still in print, do not receive great popular or critical attention. He himself thought he was a poet first and novelist second and volumes of poetry appeared over a period of nearly sixty years. Probably his best known poem is *Modern Love*, an innovative work which covers the disillusionment and unhappiness of a doomed marriage, a subject which Meredith, whose first wife decamped with the painter Henry Wallis, knew intimately.

Selected Poems
Carcanet pbk £6.95

extraordinary metrical and verbal innovations. Even thirty years after his death Hopkins' 'sprung rhythm', a method of scanning verse by accent or stress rather than
by the counting of syllables, seemed bewildering to readers but his reputation as a major poet was steadily recognised in the twenties and thirties.

Poems and Prose
Penguin pbk £5.99

Poems
Oxford UP pbk £9.99

God's Grandeur
by Gerard Manley Hopkins

The world is charged with the grandeur of God.
It will flame out, like shining from shook foil;
It gathers to a greatness, like the ooze of oil
Crushed. Why do men then now not reck his rod?
Generations have trod, have trod, have trod;
And all is seared with trade; bleared, smeared with toil;
And wears man's smudge and shares man's smell: the soil
Is bare now, nor can foot feel, being shod.

And for all this, nature is never spent;
There lives the dearest freshness deep down things;
And though the last lights off the black West went
Oh, morning, at the brown brink eastward, springs -
Because the Holy Ghost over the bent
World broods with warm breast and with ah! bright wings.

Morris, William
(1834 - 1896)

The son of a prosperous businessman, Morris was one of the great figures of Victorian culture, a man of diverse enthusiasms, talents and achievements. After Oxford he trained originally as an architect but his growing hatred of industrial production and the alienation of the worker from his work led him to found, together with friends such as Rossetti and Burne-Jones, a firm dedicated to the production of furniture, printed textiles, tapestries, wallpapers and stained glass.

Drawing of Christina Rossetti
by Dante Gabriel Rossetti

The firm's work over several decades revolutionised public taste in design but Morris, a man of volcanic energies, also found time to become one of the leading figures in English socialism, to write several Utopian fantasies, to undertake translations of classic literature and of the Norse sagas and to establish the Kelmscott Press for the printing of fine books. He wrote poetry throughout his adult life and his first volume *The Defence of Guinevere* was a product of his love for Arthurian literature.

The Earthly Paradise, published in three volumes between 1868 and 1870, was a dreamlike evocation of a world, part Norse, part Greek, untainted by the horrors of industrial society and its appeal to the Victorian middle classes was such that Morris was established as one of the most popular poets of the period.

Selected Poetry
Carcanet pbk £8.95

Rossetti, Christina
(1830 - 1894)

Sister to Dante Gabriel and William Michael Rossetti, two of the founder members of the Pre-Raphaelite Brotherhood, Christina Rossetti shared many of the aesthetic aims of her brothers and her early poetry was published in *The Germ*, the house magazine of the PRB. Later work such as *Goblin Market*, a strange fairy tale open to interpretation as both psychosexual revelation and religious allegory, retains something of the Pre-Raphaelite atmosphere. However her sense of melancholy and mystical yearning and her considerable technical virtuosity give her a very distinctive voice as a poet, one that has had considerable appeal to readers and fellow poets in the years since her death.

Selected Poems
Carcanet pbk £5.95

Choice of Christina Rossetti's Verse
Faber pbk £5.99

Remember
by Christina Rossetti

Remember me when I am gone away,
Gone far away into the silent land;
When you can no more hold me by the hand,
Nor I half turn to go yet turning stay.
Remember me when no more day by day
You tell me of our future that you planned:
Only remember me; you understand
It will be late to counsel then or pray.
Yet if you should forget me for a while
And afterwards remember, do not grieve:
For if the darkness and corruption leave
A vestige of the thoughts that once I had,
Better by far you should forget and smile
Than that you should remember and be sad.

Dante Gabriel Rossetti by Holman Hunt

Rossetti, Dante Gabriel
(1828 - 1882)

Born into a family of Italian political exiles, Rossetti was drawn early to an artistic career and was one of the founder members of the Pre-Raphaelite Brotherhood. As both poet and painter Rossetti was a dominant figure in the movement throughout the 1850s, the period of his doomed relationship with Lizzie Siddall, whose death from an overdose of laudanum in 1862 affected him so deeply that he buried the manuscripts of many of his poems with her. In the years following Siddall's death his painting was increasingly secondary to his work in the decorative arts - he was a member of William Morris' firm - and then, as eyestrain developed, he turned more and more to poetry. In a bizarre episode he exhumed Siddall's body to rescue his manuscript poems, some of which were published in a collection of 1870. Soon after this he was the subject of a vitriolic critical attack accusing him and his associates ('the Fleshly School of Poetry', as the critic dubbed them) of impurity and obscenity. Rossetti responded vigorously but ill-health was taking its toll on him and he became increasingly reclusive in his last years. Rossetti's poetry, turning constantly to times past and to Arthurian legend, can be irritating to a modern sensibility but there is no doubt that his own particular version of late Romanticism was an important component of Victorian culture.

**Selected Poems
and Translations**
Carcanet pbk £5.95

Swinburne, Algernon
(1837 - 1909)

The son of an admiral, Swinburne was brought up in the Isle of Wight and educated at Eton. At Oxford he moved in the Pre-Raphaelite circles of Rossetti and he gained early celebrity with the poetic drama *Atalanta in Calydon*. In 1866 he published *Poems and Ballads* and immediately exchanged celebrity for notoriety. The themes of moral and spiritual rebellion, combined with a flirtation with the sadistic and the sexually ambiguous, which characterise the poems proved too strong for Victorian taste and Swinburne was memorably described by one critic as 'the libidinous laureate of a pack of satyrs'. Meanwhile Swinburne was making his own descent into alcoholism from which he was only rescued in 1879 by the intervention of an admirer, Theodore Watts-Dunton, who carried him off to the more sedate suburban pleasures of Putney where he lived, together with Watts-Dunton, for the rest of his life. Swinburne's importance as an imaginative user of old forms and his brave experimentation with subject matter, which point forward from high Victorianism to *fin de siècle*, are noteworthy but his own verbal and poetic fluency often betray him into an overwrought lushness which he himself described as 'a tendency to the dulcet and luscious form of verbosity which has to be guarded against.'

Selected Poems
Carcanet pbk £7.95

Tennyson, Alfred
LORD (1809 - 1892)

The third surviving son of a Lincolnshire rector, Tennyson was one of a large, talented and highly neurotic family, a family haunted by violence, epilepsy and alcoholism. He went on to become Poet Laureate and an embodiment of what have since come to be known as Victorian values. His period at Cambridge ended without him taking a degree but, in his time there, he met A.H. Hallam, the friend whose early death in 1833 moved Tennyson to write *In Memoriam*, the central poem in his oeuvre and in the entire spectrum of Victorian poetry, the poem which best exemplifies the anxieties and forebodings of the age. As T. S. Eliot wrote of the poem 'It is not religious because of the quality of its faith, but because of the quality of its doubt. Its faith is a poor thing, but its doubt is a very intense experience.' *In Memoriam* was finally published in 1850 (he had earlier broken a long poetic silence with volumes which included such well known verses as *The Lady of Shalott* and *The Lotos Eaters*) and 1850 was Tennyson's *annus mirabilis* in which he was also married to Emily Sellwood to whom he had been engaged for many years and was confirmed in the status of Poet Laureate. From this year on the transformation of Tennyson into the bearded and patriarchal bard, familiar from portraits and memoirs, was underway. The poetry continued to pour forth. *Maud*, published in 1855, contained some of his best lyrics and 1859 saw the publication of the first four *Idylls of the King*. His rendition of the Arthurian legends was finally concluded in the 1870s but he continued to be poetically active to the end, although there were increasing instances of his muse nodding. Tennyson's reputation has fallen and risen again in the century since his death - even in the last twenty years of his life admiring estimations were being revised - and it is now generally considered that his gifts were better suited to the lyric than to the epic narrative verse to which he devoted so much energy.

In Memoriam, Maud and Other Poems
Dent pbk £4.99

Idylls of the King
Penguin pbk £9.99

Poems and Plays
Oxford UP pbk £11.99

Selected Poems
Penguin pbk £6.99

Wilde, Oscar
(1854 - 1900)

The tragedy of Wilde's spectacular fall from grace - from the feted author of epigrammatic comedies to the victim of prosecution and imprisonment for homo-sexuality, from lionisation by London society to confinement in Reading gaol, exile and early death - is well known. His poetry is largely derivative and unoriginal, a criticism that could be levelled at most of the poetry of the *fin de siècle*. The exception is *The Ballad of Reading Gaol*, published after his release from prison, which is an understandably overcharged but nonetheless moving account of his experiences.

Selected Poems
Carcanet pbk £6.95

Illustration by A. Beardsley for Wilde's *Salome*

20th Century Verse

Abse, Dannie
(1923 -)

Abse was born in Wales into a Jewish family and has spent his working life as a doctor. These biographical facts are often reflected in his accessible and discursive writings, both poetry and prose. His *Collected Poems,* published in 1989, demonstrate his skill in creating over more than forty years his own compassionate and wryly humorous poetic voice.

White Coat, Purple Coat
Hutchinson pbk £9.99

Selected Poems
Penguin pbk £6.99

Adcock, Fleur
(1934 -)

Although she was born and educated in New Zealand, Fleur Adcock has spent much of her working life, and her life as a poet, in London and some of her poetry, in its interest in questions of identity and rootedness, reflects this dual allegiance to place. Her verse is unsentimental in its clear-eyed view of personal relationships and her poised ironies often mask a rather chilling quality as she examines the deceptions of love. Her *Selected Poems* brings together poetry from a number of separate collections. She has also worked extensively as an anthologist and translator.

Selected Poems
Oxford UP pbk £7.99

Alvi, Moniza
(1954 -)

One of the poets chosen for the 'New Generation Poets' promotion in 1994, Moniza Alvi has published two collections heavily influenced by time spent in India and Pakistan, her birthplace. Allied to this are thoughts and echoes of her upbringing in England. Through richly multicultural poems Alvi maps out her territory of childhood, family, identity and the strangeness of rediscovery. The Pakistan she left as a small child is vividly portrayed in the collection *The Country at my Shoulder.*

A Bowl of Warm Air
Oxford UP pbk £6.99

The Country at my Shoulder
Oxford UP pbk £6.99

Simon Armitage

photo Jason Bell

Armitage, Simon
(1963-)

Simon Armitage shot to prominence with his first collection *Zoom*. His reputation as the most widely and unreservedly praised poet of his generation has been confirmed by subsequent books which include *Kid* and *The Dead Sea Poems*. He has also published his verse accompaniments to TV films which he has made. Armitage is remarkable for his originality, versatility and confidence. His voice, which transforms the vernacular, creates, to startling effect, a tough muscular lyric cut through with tenderness.

Book of Matches
Faber pbk £6.99

The Dead Sea Poems
Faber pbk £6.99

Kid
Faber pbk £6.99

Zoom
Bloodaxe pbk £6.95

The Winner
by Simon Armitage

When the feeling went in the lower half of my right arm
they fitted a power-tool into the elbow joint
with adjustable heads. When I lost the left
they gave me a ball on a length of skipping rope
and I played the part of a swingball post
on a summer lawn for a circle of friends.
After the pins and needles in my right leg
they grafted a shooting-stick onto the stump.
When septicaemia took the other peg
I thanked the mysterious ways of the Lord
for the gift of sight and my vocal cords.
With the brush in my teeth, I painted Christmas cards.
When I went blind, they threaded light-bulbs
into the sockets, and slotted a mouth-organ
into the groove of the throat when cancer struck.
For ears, they kitted me out with a baby's sock
for one, and a turned out pocket, sellotaped on.

Last autumn I managed the Lyke Wake Walk,
forty-odd miles in twenty-four hours - oh Ma,
treasure this badge that belongs to your son
with his nerves of steel and his iron will.
This Easter I'm taking the Life Saving Test - oh Pa,
twenty five lengths of the baths towing a dead weight,
picture your son in his goggles and vest, with a heart
like a water-pump under a battleship chest.

Ash, John
(1948 -)

Ash is a Manchester-born poet now living in New York whose chief source of literary inspiration has been the more experimental strains of French and American poetry. His more recent work, 'urban pastoral', as Ash himself described it, also shows the influence of friend and mentor John Ashbery.

Disbelief
Carcanet pbk £6.95

Auden, W. H.
(1907 - 1973)

At Oxford, where his contemporaries included Spender, Louis MacNeice and C. Day-Lewis, Auden was already making a name as a poet and, when his first major collection was published by Faber in 1930, he was immediately established as the most distinctive voice in the generation of left wing poets of the Thirties. This was a position he was to hold

W.H Auden

throughout the decade as he produced further collections, wrote several plays in collaboration with Christopher Isherwood and undertook brief service as an ambulance driver in the Spanish Civil War, which resulted in the long poem *Spain*. In 1939 Auden, together with Isherwood, left for the United States where he lived for many years and met Chester Kallman who was to be his companion until his death. He became a US citizen in 1946. The poetry Auden wrote after his arrival in the States, published in collections such as *New Year Letter* and *The Shield of Achilles*, moved away from what he came to see as the simplifications of his Thirties' beliefs and increasingly towards the Anglicanism and Christian beliefs in which he had been brought up. Auden's influence on his own and succeeding generations of poets was enormous and the complexity and range of his work, together with his mastery of verse form, proved an exacting model. His poetry has recently gained an unexpected boost in sales after the use of one of his love lyrics in the film *Four Weddings and a Funeral*.

Selected Poems
Faber pbk £8.99

Collected Poems
Faber pbk £15.99

Collected Shorter Poems
Faber pbk £9.99

Barker, George
(1913 - 1991)

Barker's first publications were in the Thirties and his poetry partook of the political concerns of the times - particularly the Spanish Civil War - and the imaginative influence of surrealism. However he is best known as one of the chief progenitors, together with Dylan Thomas, of the wartime movement, the New Apocalypse, a neo-romantic, wildly rhetorical reaction to what was seen as the 'classicism' of Auden and his contemporaries. His later work includes a startling self-presentation in verse, *The True Confession of George Barker,* and several volumes in the seventies and eighties of verse more relaxed and elegiac than his previous work.

Selected Poems
Faber pbk £8.99

Bell, Martin
(1918 - 1978)

Bell's poetry, often drawing on his experiences as soldier and as schoolteacher, was largely written in the fifties and sixties when he was a senior member of the circle of poets known as the Group. The only volume he published in his lifetime was a *Collected Poems,* which appeared in 1967, but since his death a more substantial volume, which incorporates later work, has appeared. He has been described by Peter Porter, who edited this, as 'one of the major poets writing in English in the second half of the century'.

Complete Poems
Bloodaxe pbk £7.95

Beer, Patricia
(1924 -)

Devon and the West Country where Patricia Beer was born and grew up, its folklore and legends, are important presences in her poetry. Her work, unobtrusively skilful in its deployment of language and metre, ranges through a wide variety of personal and historical subject matter but returns time and again, almost obsessively, to the theme of mortality, the insecurity that haunts even the most apparently comfortable of lives. She has also written several significant works of criticism.

Collected Poems
Carcanet pbk £6.95

Berry, James
(1924 -)

James Berry was one of the first immigrants from the Caribbean to settle in Britain after the war and his work reflects his experience of being black in Britain and his attempts to integrate what he values in both Jamaican and British culture. He draws skilfully on Jamaican dialect and folktales in his writings, which also include a number of books for children and anthologies of black poetry.

Hot Earth Cold Earth
Bloodaxe pbk £8.95

Betjeman, John
(1906 - 1984)

Betjeman was born in Highgate into a family of Dutch origin and his childhood is minutely recalled in his verse autobiography *Summoned by Bells.* His collections of verse, appearing from the early thirties, soon gained an unusually wide audience and his *Collected Poems,* published in 1958, was reprinted many times, selling close to a million copies. This popular readership, and the apparent simplicity of Betjeman's verse, have led to him being dismissed by many critics. However fellow poets such as Auden and Larkin admired his work and the simplicity is deceptive - Betjeman was a sophisticated manipulator of regular rhythms and well-worn rhymes for ironic purposes and his apparently cheerful, if satiric, celebrations of middle class life and of a certain strain of Englishness are shot through with melancholy and fear of death. He was Poet Laureate from 1972 until his death.

Best of Betjeman
Penguin pbk £6.99

Collected Poems
John Murray pbk £10.99

Summoned by Bells
John Murray pbk £9.95

The Harbour
by Eavan Boland

This harbour was made by art and force
and called Kingstown and afterwards Dun Laoghaire
and holds the sea behind its barrier
less than five miles from my house.

City of shadows and of the gradual
capitulations to the last invader
this is the final one: signed in water
and witnessed in granite and ugly bronze and gun metal.

Lord be with us say the makers of a nation.
Lord look down say the builders of a harbour.
They came and cut a shape out of ocean
and left stone to close around their labour.

Officers and their wives promenaded
once on this spot and saw with their own eyes
the opulent horizon and obedient skies
which nine tenths of the law provided.

Frigates with thirty-six guns cruising
the outer edges of influence could idle
and enter here and catch the tide of
empire and arrogance and the Irish sea rising.

And rising through a century of storms
and cormorants and moonlight all along this coast
while an ocean forgot an empire and the armed
ships under it changed to salt and rust :

A seagull with blue and white and grey feathers
swoops down and rolls and finishes
its flight overhead and vanishes -
its colours stolen where the twilight gathers.

Blunden, Edmund
(1896 - 1974)
Blunden's life and writings were
shaped by his experiences in the
trenches during World War I.
Many of the finest poems to
emerge from the conflict, such
as *Third Ypres* and *Report on
Experience* are his and his prose
memoir *Undertones of War* ranks
with Robert Graves' better known
Goodbye to All That as a description of the destruction of man
and landscape in Flanders. In
later life he was a critic and
university teacher and produced
editions of the work of his fellow
war poets Wilfred Owen and Ivor
Gurney as well as an edition of
Clare which pioneered the
rediscovery of that poet.

Selected Poems
Carcanet pbk £6.95

Boland, Eavan
(1944 -)

Perhaps Ireland's foremost
woman poet, Boland has shown
an ability in her work to
accommodate themes of Irish
identity and history, the legacies
of oppression and colonialism,
together with an ability to
address questions about the
marginalisation of women and
to write of the personal and
the lyric. Her *Collected Poems,*
published in 1995, draws on a
number of previous collections
from her first in 1967 to the
present day.

Collected Poems
Carcanet pbk £9.95

Selected Poems
Carcanet pbk £5.95

Brackenbury, Alison
(1953-)

Alison Brackenbury was born in Lincolnshire, educated at Oxford and now lives and works in Gloucestershire. Her poetry, published in a number of collections since her first major volume appeared in 1981, shows a range and technical facility that place her amongst the most considerable poets of her generation. Her *Selected Poems* displays the variety of her subject matter, from poems rooted in particular landscapes to dramatic monologue, from explorations of ordinary, provincial lives to short love lyrics.

Selected Poems
Carcanet pbk £6.95

Alison Brackenbury

Brooke, Rupert
(1887 - 1915)

Before the outbreak of the First World War, Brooke was known as the leader of the intellectual *jeunesse dorèe* of the period and an important contributor to the first and second volumes of *Georgian Poetry*, an anthology published intermittently between 1912 and 1922. After the war began Brooke rapidly joined up and in early 1915 he published his five War Sonnets. These included *The Soldier* ('If I should die, think only this of me') which immediately raised Brooke to the position of a national and patriotic icon, a position only confirmed by his death from blood-poisoning on the way to the Dardanelles. His reputation suffered dramatically as the old certainties about country and empire eroded but some of his lighter verse, including the well-known *The Old Vicarage, Grantchester,* is highly accomplished.

Collected Poems
Macmillan pbk £11.00

Poetical Works of Rupert Brooke
Faber pbk £6.99

Brown, George Mackay
(1921 -)

As a novelist, George Mackay Brown was shortlisted for the Booker prize in 1994. As a poet he has been publishing verse since the fifties, all of it deeply influenced by the landscapes, ways of life and folklore of his native Orkney. His poetry, independent and indifferent to passing fashion, has won much praise from his fellow poets. Seamus Heaney has written that 'his sense of the world and his way with words are powerfully at one with each other.'

Following a Lark
John Murray pbk £8.99

Selected Poems 1954 - 1992
John Murray pbk £8.99

Bunting, Basil
(1900 - 1985)

Born in Northumberland, Bunting worked as an editor on Transatlantic Review in Paris, was a friend and disciple of Ezra Pound and led a peripatetic life through Europe, the Middle East and elsewhere before returning after the Second World War to Newcastle where he worked as a journalist. He published in Europe and America and gained a reputation among younger American poets as a significant figure in the modernist movement but he was virtually unknown in Britain before the publication of *Briggflatts* in 1966. This extraordinary long poem, defining and celebrating a Northumbrian community, its language and history, immediately established him as the major English poet of the century to have digested and recast the example of Pound.

Complete Poems
Oxford UP pbk £10.99

Burnside, John
(1955 -)

Since the publication of his first collection in 1989, Burnside has published four further volumes which have established his reputation as one of Britain's finest poets. The poet and critic Adam Thorpe has gone so far as to say, 'If genius is operating anywhere in English poetry at present, I feel it is here, in Burnside's singular music.' His earlier collection *The Myth of the Twin* was shortlisted for the T. S. Eliot Prize and his most recent volume *Swimming in the Flood*, published in 1995, is further proof of his capacity to create a mysterious world, parallel to our mundane one, in which the lost and the damaged move towards some form of recovery and renewal.

The Myth of the Twin
Cape pbk £7.00

Swimming in the Flood
Cape pbk £7.00

Anstruther
by John Burnside

Watching the haar move in
I think of the times we came out here, as children,

and disappeared like ghosts
into the fog :

ghosts for ourselves, at least; we were still
involved with substance

and swallows flickering along the rim
of light and sand

avoided us, no matter how we tried
to be invisible.

The far shore, that I used to think
was somewhere strange,

the lighthouse that once seemed large
and fishing boats beneath the harbour wall

are forming anew
within this caul of mist,

more real than ever, harder and more precise,
and nothing ghostly in the way

the cold welds to my skin
and lets me know

how quick I am, how quick I have to be
to go on walking, blindly, into silence.

Cameron, Norman
(1905 - 1953)

During his lifetime Cameron published only two collections but his carefully crafted verses, often built around a single, fluently developed metaphor, were much admired by fellow poets, including Robert Graves and Dylan Thomas. He worked as a translator and his *Collected Poems* include versions of Heine, Nerval and Villon.

Collected Poems
Anvil pbk £14.95

Carson, Ciaran
(1948 -)

Born into an Irish-speaking family in Belfast and educated at Queen's University there, Carson published his first collection in 1976 and it was described by Tom Paulin as evidence of a 'brilliant and formidable talent'. However it was to be more than ten years before his second collection, *The Irish for No,* appeared, although it was in this collection and the volume *Belfast Confetti* that his mature voice emerged. Carson's handling of the long line in his verse, which appears to meander but is, in reality, carefully controlled, is highly distinctive and he uses it skilfully to encompass the narratives, anecdotes and histories with which he memorialises his troubled native city.

Belfast Confetti
Bloodaxe pbk £6.95

Opera Et Cetera
Blodaxe pbk £7.95

Causley, Charles
(1917 -)

Causley, who has lived and worked in Cornwall for much of his life, has produced many volumes of poetry both for adults and for children. His work, often incorporating modern concerns into traditional verse forms, particularly the ballad, aims at accessibility and readability and has gained a wide audience. His *Collected Poems* gathers together verses from more than forty years which demonstrate his command of language and imagery, his gentle humour and his ability to renew the power of long-established verse forms.

Collected Poems
Macmillan pbk £15.00

Clarke, Gillian
(1937 -)

Gillian Clarke has lived in South Wales for most of her life and her various collections have established her place among the leading Welsh poets of her generation. Her poems, often descriptions of the natural world and apparently simple evocations of family and social life, have an unforced capacity to move from the particular to the larger themes of life and death, love and loss and she writes with especial strength about women's experiences through the centuries.

Selected Poems
Carcanet pbk £5.95

The King of Britain's Daughter
Carcanet pbk £6.95

Clemo, Jack
(1916 - 1994)

Once described as 'one of the strangest and most original writers of our time', Jack Clemo was born in Cornwall, the son of a clay-kiln worker, and lived there all his life, often as a virtual recluse in an isolated granite cottage. He was deaf from an early age and lost his sight completely in 1955. He published two visionary novels in the years immediately after the war. His intense poetry is dominated by the austere landscape in which much of it was written and in which Clemo conducted what he described as his 'terrible wrestle with God'. His later writings move from the puritanical hatred of the natural world, which is only too evident in the earlier collections, towards a mellower reconciliation to the human condition, a development Clemo himself ascribed to the humanising effects of his late marriage in 1968.

Selected Poems
Bloodaxe pbk £6.95

The Cured Arno
Bloodaxe pbk £6.95

Cope, Wendy
(1945 -)

Wendy Cope was a teacher for a number of years after graduating from Oxford. The success of her two collections, which both reached the bestseller lists, has established her as possibly the most popular poet in the country. Her skill in manipulating traditional verse forms for parodic purposes is considerable and her slyly subversive view of social behaviour is refreshing.

Making Cocoa for Kingsley Amis
Faber pbk £6.99

Serious Concerns
Faber pbk £5.99

Wendy Cope

Crawford, Robert
(1959 -)

Crawford, who has written poetry in both English and Scots, has been a significant figure in recent literary attempts to map out a regenerated Scottish cultural identity and his first two collections were notable for their engagement, positive but not uncritical, with Scottish themes. His most recent work, *Masculinity,* is a more autobiographical collection in which Crawford explores his own childhood, marriage and fatherhood. As the title makes clear, the poetry is also concerned with the politics and rhetoric of gender and with the formulation of viable definitions of masculinity, framed in Crawford's lively and often amusing language.

Masculinity
Cape pbk £7.00

Dabydeen, David
(1955 -)

David Dabydeen was born in Guyana, educated in Cambridge and London and has pursued a career as an academic as well as a poet and novelist. His interest in language and the ways in which forms of English carry political and social messages not superficially apparent is reflected in his poetry which has made striking use of the dialect of his native Guyana and explored the lives of people isolated, socially and linguistically, from the mainstream of British life. His most recent collection *Turner* centres on Turner's painting The Slave Ship, responding imaginatively and liberatingly to it.

Turner
Cape pbk £7.00

D'Aguiar, Fred
(1960 -)

D'Aguiar was born in London of Guyanese parents and spent his childhood in Guyana before returning to Britain in the seventies. He has published fiction as well as poetry and edited anthologies of black British verse. His own poetry uses Creole dialect to great effect and is particularly vivid in its depiction of his childhood and the network of family relations within which he grew up.

British Subjects
Bloodaxe pbk £5.95

Davie, Donald

(1922 -1995)

Davie was born in Yorkshire and educated at Cambridge where he came under the influence of Leavis, who underpinned the strong sense of the ethical importance of literature and poetry which he had imbibed during his Baptist upbringing. Davie went on to a successful career in academic life and, in his critical work *Purity of Diction in English Verse,* wrote what could be seen as the manifesto of the fifties Movement poets. Davie's own poetry is possessed of many of the virtues of the best Movement poetry - precision, sceptical and ironic commonsense, accomplished reworking of traditional forms and metres - and his own commitment to the reading and translation of other, particularly East European, literatures meant that he never fell victim to the narrowness and parochialism of some Movement poets.

Selected Poems
Carcanet pbk £5.95

Poems and Melodramas
Carcanet pbk £7.95

Donald Davie

photo Doreen Davie

Bits and Pieces
by Donald Davie

Harmonious first and last,
a classical composure,
is what the republican mentors
ask of a verse in your honour.

For them to accredit it,
bits here and pieces there
knocked together aren't
sufficiently severe.

And no doubt they are right.
Clear-eyed accommodations
don't measure up to our sessions;
neither do porticos.

Composites, inspired
improvisations on
the one part and the other,
make up the script of our love.

Ah my Isotta, I'd
raise you a temple not
less ramshackle than
the one in Rimini.

Deane, Seamus

(1940 -)

Born in Derry, Seamus Deane is a writer and academic who has published a number of books of literary criticism, a novel *Reading in the Dark,* and several volumes of poetry. His poetry, like all his writings, is intense and serious, marked by a sharp intelligence and evidence of wide reading.

Political and social themes predominate, although they are always addressed with formal elegance and emotional restraint, and while his work is thick with historical facts, he leads the reader through to his conclusions without obfuscation. Again and again he returns to the sectarian violence of modern Ireland, frequently via historical or literary juxtapositions. In *History Lessons,* the title poem of his third collection, the Napoleonic and Hitlerian assaults on Moscow serve as a context for the 'Elections, hunger-strikes and shots' of contemporary Northern Ireland.

Selected Poems
Gallery Press pbk £5.95

De La Mare, Walter
(1873 - 1956)

De La Mare's poetry for both adults and children, of which he published many volumes, has not always been fashionable but has remained consistently popular. His verse, often dealing in fantasy and in the mysteries lurking behind the apparently commonplace, shows much technical inventiveness and was admired even by writers as different in outlook as T. S. Eliot and Graham Greene. He was also the author of a number of idiosyncratic prose works (*Memoirs of a Midget* is a bizarrely created 'auto-biography' of a minute Miss M.) and editor of highly successful anthologies, some of which remain in print.

Collected Poems
Faber pbk £14.99

Collected Rhymes and Verses
Faber pbk £8.99

Selected Poems
Faber pbk £6.99

Douglas, Keith
(1920 - 1944)

Douglas was killed during the Normandy invasion and inevitably he is remembered chiefly as a war poet, one whose work faces the prospect of imminent death without recourse to false rhetoric and sentimentality. The enthusiasm of Ted Hughes, among others, who wrote an introduction to a selection of his verses in the sixties, brought him to a new audience. His vivid narrative of the war in North Africa, *From Alamein to Zem Zem,* was published posthumously.

Complete Poems
Oxford UP pbk £8.99

Duffy, Carol Ann
(1955 -)

Carol Ann Duffy has been described as 'one of the freshest and bravest talents to emerge in British poetry, in any poetry, for years.' She has won many prizes for her work including the Whitbread and the Forward for her last collection *Mean Time* which was also shortlisted for the T.S. Eliot prize in 1993. Her dramatic talent (she has written a number of works for the theatre) is often directed into powerful character monologues which are presented alongside passionate love poems which she writes, as Robert Nye has remarked, 'as if she were the first to do so.' Duffy's work artfully balances social realism, psychological insight and romance.

Mean Time
Anvil Press pbk £5.95

Selected Poetry
Penguin pbk £5.95

Dunmore, Helen
(1952 -)

Born in Yorkshire and educated at the University of York, Dunmore has published several collections since the appearance of her first, *The Apple Fall,* in 1983 and she has also recently turned successfully to the writing of fiction. Her third novel *A Spell in Winter* won the first Orange Prize for fiction in 1996 amidst some publicity. Dunmore's verse demonstrates her strong visual sense and her confident use of rhythm and sound has been apparent from the first. Her success in fusing the domestic and the miniature with larger themes of contemporary culture and politics is noteworthy.

Recovering a Body
Bloodaxe pbk £6.95

Short Days, Long Nights: New & Selected Poems
Bloodaxe pbk £7.95

Candle Poem
by Helen Dunmore (after Mahmoud Darwish)

A candle for the ship's breakfast
eaten while moving southward
through mild grey water
with the work all done,
a candle for the house seen from outside,
the voices and shadows
of the moment before coming home,

a candle for the noise of aeroplanes
going elsewhere, passing over,
for delayed departures, embarrassed silences
between people who love one another,
a candle for sandwiches in service stations
at four am, and the taste of coffee
from plastic cups, thickened with sugar
to keep us going,

a candle for the crowd around a coffin
and the terrible depth it has to fall
into the grave dug for everyone,
the deaths for decades to come,
our deaths ; a candle for going home
and feeling hungry after saying
we would never be able to eat the ham,
the fruit cake, those carefully-buttered buns.

Durcan, Paul
(1944 -)

Born in Dublin, Durcan has produced numerous collections since his first fully-fledged volume appeared, to great acclaim, in 1975. His poetry combines what one critic has called 'an open romanticism rare in contemporary poetry' with polemical and satirical social commentary, often using bizarrely humorous juxtapositions and whimsical titles. His use of apparently conversational language, although a language that cleverly confounds the reader's expectations, and his humour have made him a popular reader of his work. Recent collections have included a number of poems in response to paintings in the National Galleries of Ireland and Britain.

Berlin Wall Cafe
Harvill pbk £6.99

Snail in My Prime
Harvill pbk £7.99

Dunn, Douglas
(1942 -)

Dunn worked as a librarian at the University of Hull with Philip Larkin and his first collection *Terry Street*, with its colloquial evocations of working class life in the town, was seen as inhabiting the same poetic territory as that of his colleague. His later collections have shown an ability to widen the political and personal range of his verse and the moving *Elegies*, a poetic embodiment of his grief at the death of his wife, was accorded particularly high praise. He has also published a verse translation of Racine's *Andromaque* and several volumes of short stories.

Elegies
Faber pbk £6.99

Selected Poems 1964 - 1983
Faber pbk £5.99

Eliot, T.S.
(1888 - 1965)

Born in St. Louis, Missouri, Eliot studied at Harvard and then spent time in Germany and at the Sorbonne before settling in England in his mid-twenties. His first collection *Prufrock and Other Observations* was published in 1917, although the title poem *The Love Song of J. Alfred Prufrock* had been published two years earlier in the influential little magazine *Poetry*. The publication in 1922 of *The Waste Land,* perhaps the single most analysed poem of the century, established his reputation decisively and it soon came to be accepted as a central text of modernism. His poetry after *The Waste Land* became increasingly religious in tendency - famously he described himself as 'classical in literature, royalist in politics and Anglo-Catholic in religion' - and this culminated in the major achievement of *Four Quartets,* a group of four long poems, each rooted firmly in a particular place and together forming a devotional sequence linked by the common themes of consciousness and memory and the individual's relationship to time. Eliot also made great efforts to revive poetic drama in such plays as *The Cocktail Party* and *Murder in the Cathedral* and was an exceptionally influential critic, pioneering the appreciation of the metaphysical poets and of a number of Elizabethan and Jacobean dramatists. As a director of Faber & Faber, he was largely responsible for building up a list of poets which represented the mainstream of the modern movement in Britain and his importance as a cultural authority in the last thirty years of his life can scarcely be exaggerated. Since his death his influence has waned and critical reassessment of his work has been undertaken but it is unlikely to undermine significantly his position in 20th century poetry.

Collected Poems 1909 -1962
Faber pbk £8.99

Four Quartets
Faber £5.99

Old Possum's Book of Practical Cats
Faber pbk £4.99

Selected Poems
Faber pbk £6.99

The Waste Land and Other Poems
Faber pbk £5.99

Enright, D.J.
(1920 -)

In his academic career, begun after taking his degree at Cambridge, where he was taught by Leavis, Enright has spent much time abroad - in Egypt, Japan, Singapore and other parts of the Far East. This is evident in his poetry, particularly his earlier collections, in which a sense of detachment from the culture he is observing combines with an undemonstrative compassion to produce a series of ironic and quizzical reflections on human behaviour. Although Enright's principal mode of writing is ironic, this does not preclude an eloquent concern for the excluded and the disadvan-taged sounding clearly in his work. He has been productive as a critic, essayist and anthologist throughout his career.

Collected Poems
Oxford UP pbk £7.95

Ewart, Gavin
(1916 - 1995)

A precocious follower of Auden, Ewart published his first poems in the mid-thirties and his first collection in 1939. After that he published no more collections for a quarter of a century but, following the appearance of *Londoners* in 1964, he became suddenly prolific, producing many collections of largely light, comic, often erotic verse. His skill as a parodist and inventive virtuosity make his poetry invariably readable and entertaining.

Selected Poems
Hutchinson pbk £9.99

Fanthorpe, U. A.
(1929 -)

U. A. Fanthorpe resigned from her position as a teacher at Cheltenham Ladies College to become, in her own words, 'a middle-aged drop-out', working in a Bristol hospital and pursuing her ambitions as a poet. Her work is most frequently rooted in observation of everyday events, often drawn from her experiences with the patients at the hospital and her intelligence and technical assurance are at the service of a sensibility attuned to the particular and the specific.

Selected Poems
Penguin pbk £5.99

Fenton, James
(1949 -)

James Fenton was educated at Oxford where he won the Newdigate Prize for Poetry. He has travelled extensively as a political and literary journalist, freelance reporter and newspaper correspondent. In addition to his slender output of poetry his books include collections of theatre criticism, reportage and travel writing; currently he is a contributor to the New York Review of Books. His first volume, *Terminal Moraine* (1972), displayed the confident manner and facility with poetic forms that has come to characterise his work. *The Memory of War* (1982), his second collection, includes mature, understated poems where Fenton's knowledge of particular places and times informed the spare poetry with a taut eloquence. *Out of Danger* (1993), his first new collection for a decade is a successful mixture of styles and tones which features the famous political ballad, *Tiananmen*, and the verse sequence, *The Manila Manifesto*. Long awaited and greeted with considerable acclaim (it has become a commonplace to compare Fenton with Auden) the collection won the Whitbread Poetry Prize.

The Memory of War/Children of Exile
Penguin pbk £6.99

Out of Danger
Penguin pbk £7.99

Fisher, Roy
(1930 -)

Fisher has written of his native Birmingham and of the industrial landscapes of the West Midlands in verse much influenced by American jazz - he is himself a jazz pianist - and by American poetry, particularly the Black Mountain school of writers. Much of the interest in his work - witty, imaginative, anarchic in its refusal to be subject to conventional forms - lies in its revelation of an English sensibility refracted through and reshaped by exposure to a wide range of influences and to the ongoing experiments of modernism.

The Dow Low Drop
Bloodaxe pbk £8.95

Fuller, John
(1937 -)

The son of poet Roy Fuller, John Fuller has shown from his earliest collection an enviable fluency in accommodating eclectic subject matter within traditional verse forms, whether it be the sonnet, blank verse or even the limerick. His self-conscious verbal ingenuity and mastery of form leads him into the realms of pastiche but when the pastiche is as skilful and interesting as his strange poem, *The Most Difficult Position,* which deals with the quarrel between two 19th century chess players, it becomes its own justification. Fuller has also written several novels and collaborated with James Fenton on verse *jeux d'esprit.*

Stones & Fires
Chatto pbk £6.99

Fuller, Roy
(1912 - 1991)

Inevitably for a poet coming of age in the thirties, Fuller showed the influence of Auden in his earlier work. As his own voice - lucid, ironic, detached - developed, he moved beyond this influence and, in some ways, he can be seen as the poet who links the Auden generation with the later poets of the Movement. Fuller was also an adept novelist and autobiographer and was, for five years, Professor of Poetry at Oxford.

Consolation
Section pbk £6.95

Graham, W. S.
(1918 - 1986)

Born in Scotland, Graham settled in Cornwall, which provides the landscape of many of his later poems. His work often refers also to the friends he made in the community of artists around St Ives and to their paintings. His best known poem is *The Nightfishing* which powerfully uses the metaphor of a fishing expedition to illuminate his own struggle with language.

Selected Poems
Faber pbk £9.99

Graves, Robert

(1895 - 1985)

The son of A. P. Graves, an Irish essayist and poet, Robert Graves was born in London and attended an English public school. From school he went straight into the trenches of the First World War and this experience coloured his first volumes of poetry and shaped his later memoir *Goodbye to All That*. After the war he led a peripatetic life through Britain and Europe and became involved in a succession of emotional entanglements, most significantly a tempestuous relationship with the American poet Laura Riding. He settled finally in Majorca and, as he grew older, developed into the roles of magus and elder statesman of British poetry. He was Professor of Poetry at Oxford from 1961-1966. Graves' literary ouput was enormous - from historical novels to idiosyncratic studies of mythology, from children's books to criticism - but he considered himself, above all, a poet. His avoidance of identification with any group or movement enabled him to develop a highly personal voice which is seen to its greatest advantage in his love poetry, at once cynical and ardent, idealistic and erotic.

Selected Poems
Penguin pbk £6.99

Gunn, Thom

(1929 -)

Gunn wrote many of the poems in his first volume while still an undergraduate at Cambridge and he has continued to produce collections regularly in the forty years since. His most recent, *The Man with Night Sweats*, in which Gunn, himself a homosexual, included moving poetry about the AIDS epidemic, was awarded the inaugural Forward prize in 1992. He moved to North California to teach soon after leaving Cambridge and has lived in the States ever since, writing and teaching at various universities. His earliest poetry was linked to that of the Movement but the link was never strong and, after his move to America, it was clear that Gunn's influences were more eclectic and his desire to experiment with form stronger than those of any Movement poet. His work throughout forty years has been a challenging blend of formal skill with free-verse improvisation, of poetic diction with contemporary idiom. His *Collected Poems* are the work of an English sensibility radically enlarged by his long immersion in American culture.

Thom Gunn

photo Auder Gum

Collected Poems
Faber pbk £9.99

The Man with Night Sweats
Faber pbk £7.99

Gurney, Ivor
(1890 - 1937)

Trained as a musician at the Royal College of Music, Gurney was moved to poetry by his appalling experiences at Passchendaele where he was gassed and wounded. The war scarred an already troubled psyche and Gurney spent the last fifteen years of his life in the City of London Mental Hospital, where he continued to write poetry. His work, set in the Gloucestershire countryside of his childhood as well as in the trenches of Flanders, sustains a vision of rural life but in language which acknowledges the strength of the forces in league to destroy that vision.

Selected Poems
Oxford UP pbk £7.99

Hannah, Sophie
(1971 -)

Sophie Hannah was born and lives in Manchester and she first came to prominence when some of her poems were featured in an anthology of new poetry published by the Manchester-based Carcanet Press. She has since published two collections of her verse and her work has been regularly broadcast on radio. Accessible and often funny, her poetry of love and lust, of the stresses and peculiarities of modern urban life, uses traditional forms in a fresh and lively way.

**The Hero and
the Girl Next Door**
Carcanet pbk £6.95

Hotels Like Houses
Carcanet pbk £6.95

Occupational Hazard
by Sophie Hannah

He has slept with accountants and brokers,
With a cowgirl (well, someone from Heals).
He has slept with non-smokers and smokers
In commercial and cultural fields.

He has slept with book-keepers, book-binders,
Slept with auditors, florists, PAs
Child psychologists, even child minders,
With directors of firms and of plays.

He has slept with the stupid and clever.
He has slept with the rich and the poor
But he sadly admits that he's never
Slept with a poet before.

Real poets are rare, he confesses,
While it's easy to find a cashier.
So I give him some poets' addresses
And consider a change of career.

Hardy, Thomas
(1840 - 1928)

Although he wrote poetry all his adult life, Hardy was known in the nineteenth century as the novelist who wrote such works as *Far From the Madding Crowd*, *The Mayor of Casterbridge*, *Tess of the D'Urbervilles* and *Jude the Obscure*. The books were praised by many for their hard-headed portrayals of rural life but also condemned for their alleged pessimism and 'immorality' and the bitterly hostile reception of the last two novels persuaded Hardy to give up the writing of fiction. From 1898 to the end of his life he published a vast amount of poetry, including the three parts of the epic verse drama *The Dynasts* and *Satires of Circumstance, Lyrics and Reveries*, a collection of particular interest because it contains the moving elegies written after the death of his first wife in 1912. As he grew older the mantle of Grand Old Man of literature fell heavily on Hardy's shoulders and public honours were showered on him, although he lived an increasingly reclusive life in Dorchester, the centre of the area he had reinvented as Wessex in his fiction. The underlying theme of much of Hardy's best poetry is that most evident in his novels - 'the implanted crookedness of things', the sense of man struggling against indifferent forces which inflict on him the pains and ironies of life and love. His verse also reveals his strong love of the natural world and his abhorrence of affected and unnecessarily laboured poetic diction. Although he achieved no great popularity as a poet in his lifetime, Hardy's work has increasingly gathered critical acclaim since his death and he can now be seen as a major influence on the century's poetry. Indeed Donald Davie went so far as to describe him as 'the most far-reaching influence, for good or ill...in British poetry of the last fifty years'.

Hardy's Love Poems
Macmillan pbk £7.99

Selected Poems
Dent pbk £5.99

Selected Poems of Thomas Hardy
Penguin pbk £5.99

Complete Poems
Macmillan pbk £15.99

Thomas Hardy
(Oxford Authors)
Oxford UP pbk £9.95

The Self-Unseeing
Thomas Hardy

Here is the ancient floor,
Footworn and hollowed and thin,
Here was the former door
Where the dead feet walked in.

She sat here in her chair,
Smiling into the fire;
He who played stood there,
Bowing it higher and higher.

Childlike, I danced in a dream;
Blessings emblazoned that day;
Everything glowed with a gleam;
Yet we were looking away!

Harrison, Tony
(1937 -)

Born in Leeds and educated at the university there, Harrison spent some time as a lecturer in West Africa but has, for nearly thirty years, earned his living through his poetry, particularly his translations and adaptations of classical works for the theatre. More recently he has also undertaken work for television, including a controversial film version of his poem *V* - a meditation on death and class divisions written during the miners' strike and triggered by a visit to a vandalised Leeds graveyard. Harrison is a poet of contradictions - a classicist from the working class, a pessimist with a zest for life, a man of erudition who wishes to reach a larger audience than poetry usually grants. He is also a poet acutely aware that the gift that allows him to give a voice to the otherwise voiceless is also what separates him from the class from which he comes.

Selected Poems
Penguin pbk £7.99

V
Bloodaxe pbk £5.95

Heaney, Seamus
(1939 -)

Heaney received the Nobel Prize for Literature in 1995 and is widely regarded as the greatest Irish poet since Yeats. His *New Selected Poems 1966-1987* draws on eight collections through which it is possible to trace his development from the rich physicality of *Death of a Naturalist* and *Door into the Dark* to the more allegorical and meditative territory of *The Haw Lantern* in 1987. The acclaimed collections *Seeing Things* of 1991 and *The Spirit Level*, published in 1996, show Heaney balancing contemporary political reality with his continuing concern with personal and public histories.

Death of a Naturalist
Faber pbk £6.99

New Selected Poems
Faber pbk £8.99

North
Faber pbk £6.99

Seeing Things
Faber pbk £6.99

The Spirit Level
Faber pbk £6.99

John Heath-Stubbs

Heath-Stubbs, John
(1918-)

Heath-Stubbs was educated at Oxford and published his first verse in a collection of 1941 called *Eight Oxford Poets,* which also included work by Sidney Keyes. In the more than fifty years since then Heath-Stubbs has been a prolific and versatile poet who has used his wide-ranging knowledge of European literatures, of classical and Arthurian mythologies and his precise craftsmanship to fashion a body of work that places him among the most substantial poets of the time. His most recent collections have combined the dry and ironic commentary on modern life, which has always been present in his work, with an elegiac celebration of the natural world. His *Selected Poems,* drawn from numerous collections, was published in 1990.

Galileo's Salad
Carcanet pbk £7.95

Selected Poems
Carcanet pbk £6.95

Henri, Adrian
(1932-)

Together with Brian Patten and Roger McGough, Henri was one of the Liverpool poets who, emerging at much the same time as the Liverpudlian music groups formed in the wake of the Beatles' success, presented their work as a performance, a poetry to be heard by an audience rather than a poetry to be read privately. Henri's work was included in the Penguin Modern Poets volume *The Mersey Sound* which became a bestseller in 1967. Since then he has continued to issue regular collections, often illustrated by his own quirky paintings and drawings, and a *Collected Poems* appeared in 1986. Henri's poetry continues to be direct, accessible and often very funny.

Collected Poems
Allison & Busby pbk £8.99

Hill, Geoffrey
(1932 -)

From his first volume, *For the Unfallen* (1959) the poetry of Geoffrey Hill has been governed by a high seriousness both in his choice of subjects and in his attitude to creative work. Writing poetry he has defined magisterially as an 'exemplary activity'. The passion he brings to his familiar themes - music, history, religion - is rigorously controlled and highlighted by the wrought precision of his language. His vast scholarly reading and historical knowledge are openly displayed which can give an impression of coldness and remoteness from his material. Praised by Peter Porter for his 'superbly burnished' poetry, he has also been criticised by Tom Paulin for obscurantism and opacity. His influences include A. E. Housman as well as Eliot and Pound; his work can be seen as a creative confrontation between the Romantic and Modernist heritage. *Mercian Hymns* (1971), a collection of inventive prose poems, reassembling the life of the eighth century King Offa, is arguably his finest work to date.

Canaan
Penguin pbk £ 9.99

Collected Poems
Penguin pbk £ 6.99

Hill, Selima
(1945 -)

Selima Hill has published five books of poetry since her first collection in 1984 and has been described by Graham Swift as 'truly gifted. She invests mundane things with a visionary, delirious brilliance.' *A Little Book of Meat*, a narrative of a farm-raised Catholic daughter's obsession with a travelling slaughter-man, is a powerful and disturbing meditation on lust as an affliction and a gift. Her most recent book is a collection of new poems and ones selected from her previous volumes, *Trembling Hearts in the Bodies of Dogs*.

A Little Book of Meat
Bloodaxe pbk £5.95

**Trembling Hearts
in the Bodies of Dogs**
Bloodaxe pbk £8.95

Hofmann, Michael
(1957 -)

The collections Hofmann has so far published have marked him out as one of the more interesting poets of his generation. The majority of his poems are off-beat, anecdotal meditations on contemporary urban life told in a self-consciously laconic voice. He has also written memorably of his uneasy relationship, compounded of love, resentment and competitiveness, with his father, the distinguished German novelist, Gerd Hofmann, some of whose work he has translated into English.

Acrimony
Faber pbk £5.99

Corona, Corona
Faber pbk £5.99

Housman, A. E.
(1859 - 1936)

A brilliant scholar who published work on a number of classical poets and became, in 1911, Professor of Latin at Cambridge, Housman produced *A Shropshire Lad*, his collection of nature and love poems, at his own expense in 1896. In the following two decades, and particularly during the First World War, it gained critical and popular acclaim for its nostalgic evocations of the countryside and its lyric pessimism. The Georgian poets acknowledged him as a forerunner of their own rural verse. He published only one further collection, *Last Poems*, in 1922.

Collected Poems
Penguin pbk £2.99

Collected Poems and Selected Prose
Penguin pbk £8.99

Hughes, Ted
(1930 -)

Ted Hughes is a doubly rare poet. He is, even to many of his critics, unquestionably a major poet; he is also a genuinely popular poet. Since his first collection *The Hawk in the Rain* in 1957 he has been prolific; *Wolfwatching* (1989) was his fourteenth collection. In addition he has written extensively and highly successfully for children, produced a version of Seneca's *Oedipus*, written various prose works and edited, with Seamus Heaney, the bestselling anthology *The Rattle Bag*. In 1984 he accepted the position of Poet Laureate. *The Hawk in the Rain* immediately established Hughes' reputation as a poet of the natural world and the volume contrasted strongly with the urbane rationalities of the dominant Movement poets. His celebration of nature's beauty and violence became more extreme in succeeding collections as the examples of Whitman and Robinson Jeffers and D. H. Lawrence and Gerard Manley Hopkins took hold of his verse. The gnarled

photo Jane Brown

Ted Hughes

consonantal textures of his language became free of regular metres and rhyme as he attempted to appear ever more spontaneous and elemental. Tom Paulin has written of Hughes' poetic trajectory that it arose from his native dissenting culture in Yorkshire and that his art is a buried protest against the greyness of modern life and politics. Paulin has also defended Hughes' narrow thematic range by reading his portraits of nature as metaphors for large historical events such as the Reformation and the Industrial Revolution. Perhaps Hughes' most important collections are *Lupercal* (1960), *Wodwo* (1967), *Crow* (1970) and *Moortown* (1979). In 1995 Faber and Faber, his longtime publisher, issued to widespread acclaim his *New Selected Poems 1957-1994* on the occasion of his sixty-fifth birthday.

Crow
Faber pbk £5.99

The Hawk in the Rain
Faber pbk £5.99

Lupercal
Faber pbk £5.99

New Selected Poems 1957-1994
Faber pbk £7.99

Spring Love
by Elizabeth Jennings

I must accept that love will never come
As it did once - quickly and unexpected
Casting a radiance on any room

That I worked in - I could be unprotected
Because surprise was the chief element
Of love like this only at me directed

And coming to me like a sacrament
Unearned and hard to credit. Part of this
Was that for years I thought that love was meant

For other people, that it would not bless
And cherish me. I was the second child,
Awkward, competitive and thinking less

Of everything would come to me. A wild
Creature I was, searching for meaning in
The universe. I never could be mild

Or sure. I never guessed love would begin
Romantically. I was caught up in it,
Amazed, enthralled and wholly altered when

I was first kissed with passion. Now I sit
Watching Spring suggest itself. There's pain
In thinking of dead loved ones yet - O yet

I feel my blood rake in my veins again
And words unfolding with the leaves while birds
Call tentatively. Poems I knew sustain

Me as love did at first. There's a refrain
Singing within me, finding me fresh words.

Jennings, Elizabeth
(1926 -)

Jennings published her first volumes in the early fifties and she was categorised, thanks to inclusion in Robert Conquest's defining anthology *New Lines*, as a Movement poet. However Jennings' own sensibility, her individual approach to themes of love, friendship and religion, made it clear that she shared neither the academic wit nor the ironic scepticism of the other poets in the anthology. This has become even clearer in her later collections. In the collections of the sixties, poems about illness and institutions are a reflection of acute personal suffering but retain a reticence and restraint very different to the 'confessional' poetry of American contemporaries. Indeed Jennings herself has said that 'confessional' poetry seems to her a contradiction in terms and she has continued to exercise her technical skill and command of a variety of forms to explore the subjects that have always interested her - love, religious experience, memory and childhood. Her *Collected Poems* is a personal selection of the poems from many collections which she wishes to represent her work.

Collected Poems
Carcanet pbk £6.95

Selected Poems
Carcanet pbk £4.95

Johnson, Linton Kwesi
(1952 -)

Born in Jamaica, Johnson was educated in Britain and worked for a time as a political activist for black causes. His poetry, which he himself has called 'dub poetry' is rooted in the rhythms of reggae and Johnson has issued a number of recordings on Virgin and Island as well as books of his poetry. His work, belligerent and aggressive but also vital and upbeat, charts the progress of modern Britain from the perspective of a young, urban black and fiercely confronts racism, police oppression and the alienation of many blacks from a society which appears to ignore or marginalise them.

Tings an Times: Selected Poems
Bloodaxe pbk £5.95

Jones, David
(1895 - 1974)

Jones studied at art school and served as a private on the western front from 1915 - 1918, an experience which shaped his first major work *In Parenthesis,* an epic mixture of poetry and prose in which the ordeals of a modern Everyman, Private John Ball, are related to historical and chivalric antecedents. Jones joined the Catholic church in 1921, worked with Eric Gill in his communities of craftsmen and spent much creative energy on wood engraving, watercolour and illustration. His second major work, *The Anathemata,* was described by Auden as 'very probably the finest long poem written in English this century'.

In Parenthesis
Faber pbk £10.99

The Anathemata
Faber pbk £12.99

Joseph, Jenny
(1932 -)

Jenny Joseph wrote the poem *Warning* - beginning 'When I am an old woman I shall wear purple/ With a red hat which doesn't go, and doesn't suit me.' - which was voted the most popular poem by a living poet in a recently publicised poll. The popularity of this one poem, rather untypical of her work, has tended to overshadow the range and originality of the poems published in the selection which drew from work over more than twenty years. *Ghosts and other company,* her first new book of poetry since 1983, is a collection of unsettling verse centred around a poem considering the haunting and bizarre army of buried statuary at Xian which archaeologists have unearthed.

Ghosts and other company
Bloodaxe pbk £6.95

Selected Poems
Bloodaxe pbk £8.95

Joyce, James
(1882 - 1941)

Joyce's reputation as the major modernist novelist - author of *Ulysses* and *Finnegan's Wake,* the two most influential and analysed novels of the century - is unassailable. His first published volume was a collection of poetry, *Chamber Music,* published in 1907, which earned him a place in the first imagist anthology. A second collection, *Pomes Penyeach,* published after *Ulysses,* contains brief lyrics and a number of satires.

Poems and Exiles
Penguin pbk £6.99

The Poems in Verse and Prose
Kyle Cathie pbk £7.99

Kavanagh, Patrick
(1904 - 1967)

Kavanagh is now recognised as the pre-eminent Irish poet of the generation after Yeats. He was born into a small farming family and his rural upbringing provided him with the material not only for much of his finest early poetry, published in newspapers from the twenties and in a first collection in 1936, but for an autobiography *The Green Fool* and a novel *Tarry Flynn.* His move to Dublin in the late thirties, what he later described as 'the worst mistake of my life', brought him to the attention of the capital's literary establishment but also embroiled him in literary quarrels which undermined and compromised much of his writing at the time. His recovery from surgery for lung cancer in the mid-fifties heralded a renewed outpouring of poetry in his last decade. Kavanagh's realistic treatment of rural life, contrasting strongly with idealised images of the peasantry in earlier poets, has been highly influential on subsequent poets including Heaney who introduced him as a character in *Station Island.*

Selected Poems
Penguin pbk £7.99

Kay, Jackie
(1961 -)

Jackie Kay received a Forward Prize for her first collection *The Adoption Papers* which was also adapted for radio. Written in the voices of mother, birth mother and daughter, the title sequence charts the emotional territory of the adoption of a black girl by white parents from three interweaving perspectives. The result is a poetry of great depth and range. Kay's second collection *Other Lovers* continues her exploration of love and memory with, as Elizabeth Bartlett notes, the 'correct balance of craftsmanship and feeling.' Jackie Kay has also published two books of poetry for children and has written widely for stage and television.

The Adoption Papers
Bloodaxe pbk £6.95

Other Lovers
Bloodaxe pbk £6.95

Kennelly, Brendan
(1936 -)

In Ireland Brendan Kennelly - professor at Trinity College, poet, commentator on Irish politics, sometime TV quizmaster - is a media star and his recent books have been bestsellers. His early poetry was acclaimed for its directness and originality and he published a *Selected Poems* as early as 1969 but it was the publication of *Cromwell*, a series of 160 poems in which an invented hero grapples with the long shadow cast by the bogeyman of Irish history, that brought him the wide audience he now enjoys. Since then he has published *The Book of Judas*, a 400 page epic on the nature of betrayal through the realms of history and the imagination, and, most recently, *Poetry My Arse*, a dazzling and witty attack on intellectual elitism and on the posturings of some poets. Kennelly himself has written, 'A poet, living his uncertainties, is riddled with different voices, many of them in vicious conflict. The poem is the arena where these voices engage each other in open and hidden conflict, and continue to do so until they are all heard.' The many voices in Kennelly's work demand a hearing.

The Book of Judas
Bloodaxe pbk £10.95

Cromwell
Bloodaxe pbk £8.95

Poetry My Arse
Bloodaxe pbk £10.95

A Time for Voices : Selected Poems
Bloodaxe £8.95

Kinsella, Thomas
(1928 -)

Kinsella's work as translator of earlier Irish verse - he has produced a notable version of the medieval work *The Tain* - and as anthologist - he edited the *New Oxford Book of Irish Verse* - is significant and his own poetry, published over more than forty years in many pamphlets and collections, some produced by his own Peppercanister Press, has made him one of the most interesting and original Irish writers of his generation. His verse can be difficult and cryptic as he has a range of reference - to Irish history and mythology, to other mythologies and literatures, to the urban landscapes of Dublin - that makes intense demands on the reader but its powerful individuality is unmistakeable. The publication of his 400 page *Collected Poems* is a major event.

Collected Poems
Oxford UP pbk £15.00

Kipling, Rudyard
(1865 - 1936)

Kipling began his career as a journalist in India, the land of his birth, and moved to England in 1889 where he rapidly established himself in the literary world. His poems, collected initially in *Barrack Room Ballads* of 1892, show a mastery of several verse forms, most notably the dramatic monologue and the narrative ballad. Kipling was a prolific writer of short stories, novels and tales for children and in 1907 was the first English writer to receive the Nobel prize. His work has often been criticised for its jingoism but he has always had admirers who have seen the ambivalence and complexity of his responses to empire, his ironic awareness of the personal costs of the commitment to imperial ideals.

Complete Verse
Kyle Cathie pbk £10.99

Selected Poems
Penguin pbk £5.99

Kuppner, Frank
(1951 -)

Kuppner was born in Glasgow, educated in the city and has lived there ever since, 'nursing', he says, 'the impossible dream of emigrating to Edinburgh.' His poetry, mostly written in the unrhymed free-verse quatrains he has made distinctively his, has appeared in several collections since his first volume *A Bad Day for the Sung Dynasty* was published in 1984. Since then Kuppner has succeeded in creating one of the most original voices in contemporary British poetry - off-beat, often very funny, not easily categorisable. His 1994 collection was entitled *Everything is Strange* and, in Kuppner's work, this is undoubtedly true.

Everything is Strange
Carcanet pbk £8.95

Larkin, Philip
(1922 - 1985)

Larkin's poetry was first published when he was at Oxford and in the early, Yeats-influenced collection *The North Ship* but it was not until the volume *The Less Deceived,* published in 1955, that his mature voice - wry, sceptical, often colloquial - reached a wide audience. He published only two further collections in the last thirty years of his life but his ability to frame contemporary speech rhythms in unobtrusive but polished metrical form led to his considerable popularity as a poet. *High Windows,* his final volume, published in 1974, was, unusually for a book of poems, a bestseller, despite its often sombre preoccupation with death and transience. Larkin edited *The Oxford Book of Twentieth Century Verse* in 1973 and his choice, condemned by some as narrow and defiantly anti-modernist, brought the work of many little-known and unfashionable poets to the attention of readers.

Collected Poems
Faber pbk £10.99

High Windows
Faber pbk £5.99

The Less Deceived
Marvell Press pbk £4.25

The North Ship
Faber pbk £5.99

The Whitsun Weddings
Faber pbk £5.99

Lawrence, D. H.
(1885 - 1930)

Born in Nottinghamshire as the son of a coalminer, Lawrence studied at the local university and taught as an elementary school teacher before publishing his first novel in 1911. In the course of the next two decades he followed a nomadic life with his wife Frieda, moving from Cornwall to Australia, from Mexico to Italy, but still produced an enormous body of work. As well as the major novels - *Sons and Lovers, Women in Love, The Rainbow* - and the volumes of short stories and novellas, he wrote and published poetry throughout his career. Under the influence of Whitman, he wished to be unconstrained by traditional metrical forms and much of his poetry is written as 'free verse'. Lawrence's passionate moralism is as evident in his poetry as in his fiction and this can occasionally lapse into a hectoring preaching but, at its best, his verse has the immediacy and power of his finest prose.

Complete Poems
Penguin pbk £13.00

Selected Poems
Penguin pbk £5.99

Lee, Laurie
(1914 -)

Best known for *Cider with Rosie*, his nostalgic account of growing up in a Cotswold village, Laurie Lee has also published many collections of poetry which are similarly suffused with his apprehension of the natural world and the countryside of his boyhood.

Selected Poems
Penguin pbk £4.99

Levi, Peter
(1931 -)

Levi was a Jesuit priest from 1964 to 1977 when he resigned from the priesthood and married. A classical scholar, translator and archaeologist, Levi has written poetry which is varied in range and escapes a simple positioning on the map of modern poetry, although the self-reflexive procedures of Wallace Stevens have clearly influenced his explorations of perception. He also draws effectively on his wide erudition - his knowledge of the past and of contemporary European poetry - and of the insights into the elusiveness of language that he has gained from his work as a translator.

Collected Poems
Anvil Press pbk £7.95

Lewis, Alun
(1915 - 1944)

Lewis was born in South Wales and worked originally as a journalist and teacher there. He joined the army in 1940, after much internal struggle to square the idea of a just war with his pacifist conscience, and was killed in Burma four years later. His poetry includes love poems, poems which address the life lived in industrial Wales and, most recurrently, poems which deal with the pervading boredom and intermittent fears of the soldier's life.

Collected Poems
Seren Press hbk £10.95

Lochhead, Liz
(1947 -)

Lochhead's success as a performer of her own poetry is driven by her skill in the creation of memorable scenes and characters and her acute ear for the nuances of spoken language, particularly Scottish and Glaswegian voices. The collections *Dreaming Frankenstein* and *True Confessions* focus, in poems, songs and monologues that can be both lyrical and satirical, on relationships, sexual politics and the vagaries of love. *Bagpipe Muzak* contains a section of revue-like recitations and also a collection of poems and poetic narratives which dissect, with often biting irony, consumerism and the tarnished trappings of everyday life, post-communist Berlin and a Glasgow newly crowned as the cultural capital of Europe. Lochhead, unsurprisingly for a poet who shows such a sense of timing and dramatic potential in her poems and songs, has also written a number of plays.

Bagpipe Muzak
Penguin pbk £5.99

Dreaming Frankenstein
Polygon pbk £6.95

True Confessions
Polygon pbk £6.95

Logue, Christopher
(1926 -)

Logue's verse was first published in the fifties when he was living in France and he has since produced many volumes and pamphlets of poetry, often addressed, like his sixties poetry in protest against the Vietnam War, to particular social issues. Amongst his most acclaimed work are the lively and racy adaptations of some books of the Iliad which have appeared in the last ten years.

Selected Poems
Faber pbk £6.99

Longley, Michael
(1939 -)

Michael Longley was born in Belfast. He worked first as a schoolteacher and later for the Arts Council of Northern Ireland where he eventually became the Director of Literature. Since his first collection *No Continuing City* was published in 1969 his reputation has grown steadily. In 1986 Paul Muldoon included Longley in his choice of ten poets for the *Faber Book of Contemporary Irish Poetry* and *Gorse Fires* (1991) won the Whitbread Poetry Award. His most recent volume *The Ghost Orchid* was also widely praised. Although some of his best work, including his most anthologised piece *Wounds,* reflects upon the impact of the Troubles, his poetry tends to be more personal than many of his contemporaries. The large themes of love, death and nature consistently appear in his typically delicate and quirky idiom.

Ghost Orchid
Cape pbk £7.00

Gorse Fires
Secker pbk £6.99

Macbeth, George
(1932 - 1992)

George Macbeth was educated at Oxford and joined the BBC soon after graduating, working for many years as a radio producer. He left the BBC in the mid-seventies to concentrate on his writings and he published a number of novels, children's books and autobiographical works as well as collections of his poetry. His verse - inventive, dark, often blackly comic - is sometimes preoccupied with death, decay and violence, although he also wrote movingly about the breakdown of relationships and, latterly, poignant reflections on his own illness and mortality.

Collected Poems
Hutchinson pbk £10.95

MacCaig, Norman
(1910 -1996)

Born and educated in Edinburgh, MacCaig worked as a teacher and lecturer throughout his career. His earliest volumes of poetry were criticised, not least by MacCaig himself in later life, for the loose and wilful obscurity associated with the New Apocalyptic movement of the forties but he increasingly developed a voice of his own in which to make lucid and precise poetic observation. His subject matter has often been the landscape, people and traditional patterns of life in the West Highlands although he has also been able to turn his observer's eye on the urban landscapes of his native Edinburgh.

Collected Poems
Chatto pbk £9.99

MacDiarmid, Hugh
(1892 - 1978)

Hugh MacDiarmid was the pseudonym adopted by Christopher Murray Grieve and, under this name, he transformed the use of Scots as a literary language and emerged as a major figure in modern poetry. His deliberate creation of a synthetic Scots, using words he found in various dialects, in dictionaries and in the colloquial language around him, was a determined effort to free Scots poetry from what he saw as pervading sentimentality and parochial nostalgia. His major work is *A Drunk Man Looks at the Thistle,* published in 1926, in which he fashions a model of what Scotland is and could be through the slowly sobering consciousness of a man awaking on a hillside after a drinking bout. MacDiarmid's politics were Nationalist and Communist - although his belligerent personality resulted in expulsion from both parties at different times in his career - and much of his poetry in the thirties was political. His later work, only partially realised and published, was a gigantic magnum opus - a poetry that he said was to be 'full of eru-dition, expertise and ecstasy.'

Complete Poems. Vol.1
Carcanet hbk £30.00

Complete Poems. Vol 2
Carcanet hbk £30.00

Selected Poems.
Penguin pbk £8.95

MacLean, Sorley
(1911 -)

Sorley MacLean, who was born into a crofting family on the island of Raasay, is the leading Gaelic poet of the century and has done much to transform and modernise verse in that language. *From Wood to Ridge* is his collected poems in Gaelic together with his own translations of some into English.

From Wood to Ridge
Vintage pbk £8.99

MacNeice, Louis
(1907 - 1963)

MacNeice is often linked, slightly misleadingly, with Auden and Spender, his friends from Oxford, but it is thus too easy to miss the individuality which marks him out as much more than a representative thirties poet. He did collaborate with Auden on *Letters from Iceland* and his *Autumn Journal* is a long personal and political meditation on the events of the thirties. However his work was never formulaic and he was clearly suspicious of all dogmatic systems of thought, preferring to celebrate what he termed 'the drunkenness of things being various' and to

Mahon, Derek
(1941 -)

John Banville, writing in The Independent, called Derek Mahon's poem, *A Disused Shed In County Wexford,* 'the most beautiful poem produced by an Irishman since the death of Yeats'. Mahon, born in Belfast and a member of the Belfast 'Group' in the mid-sixties, under the influence of Philip Hobsbaum, is the possessor of a distinctive and masterful voice and an abundant and artful imagination. A number of his abiding themes are illustrated in *A Disused Shed* - notably, the disintegration of contemporary society and the plight of the Irish within this disorder.

Selected Poems
Penguin pbk £6.95

Masefield, John
(1878 - 1967)

Masefield is the author of some of the most familiar verse of the century - his ballad beginning 'I must go down to the sea again', for example - and was Poet Laureate from 1930 to his death but his work was critically disparaged throughout the latter part of his long life. However, recently his verse, particularly such long narrative poems as *Reynard the Fox* and *The Everlasting Mercy,* has been reassessed and his range and versatility acknowledged.

Selected Poems
Carcanet pbk £9.95

Louis MacNeice

search for his own sense of a pattern in life's flux. He worked as a producer at the BBC for many years and was also the writer of a number of innovative radio dramas and documentaries. Since his death his reputation has grown and the presence in his work of Irish themes and tones has led to his being hailed as a precursor by many of the Ulster poets of the last thirty years.

Collected Poems
Faber pbk £14.99

Selected Poems
Faber pbk £7.99

Maxwell, Glyn
(1962 -)

Born and brought up in Welwyn Garden City, Maxwell read English at Oxford and then won a scholarship to Boston University where he studied poetry and playwriting under the guidance, amongst others, of Derek Walcott. Enormous praise was rightly showered on his first collection *Tale of the Mayor's Son* when it appeared in 1990. Joseph Brodsky was moved to describe him as 'a poet of immense promise and unforgettable delivery.' Since then the prolific Maxwell has produced two further collections as well as a novel and plays and verse-dramas, some of which he has performed in the unconventional setting of the family home's back garden in Welwyn. The range and energy of his verse are vast and he has a remarkable ability to accommodate colloquial language and the rhythms of everyday speech within what are often elaborate and sophisticated verse-forms.

Out of the Rain
Bloodaxe pbk £6.95

Rest for the Wicked
Bloodaxe pbk £6.95

Tale of the Mayor's Son
Bloodaxe pbk £6.95

McGough, Roger
(1937 -)

An early success as one of the Liverpool Poets in the sixties, McGough has gone on to establish himself as one of the most prolific and popular poets in the country. His *Selected Poems* brings together examples of his lively and amusing verse from many collections. Always an accomplished performer of his work - and a founder member of the pop group the Scaffold - he continues to give regular readings of his poetry. He has also, like fellow Liverpudlian Brian Patten, written many volumes of verse for children.

Blazing Fruit :
Selected Poems 1967 - 1987
Penguin pbk £6.99

Defying Gravity
Penguin pbk £6.99

Melting into the Foreground
Penguin pbk £6.99

Middleton, Christopher
(1926 -)

Since his first major collection in 1962 Christopher Middleton has produced a body of work that is determinedly experimental, not easily categorisable in its efforts to undermine and refashion conventional poetic forms and structures. He is also a distinguished translator from German who has produced fine versions of poets as diverse as Holderlin and Paul Celan and translated contemporary German fiction and poetry.

Intimate Chronicles
Carcanet pbk £8.95

Mitchell, Adrian
(1932 -)

Mitchell was one of the pioneers of Underground Poetry in the sixties, accessible, freewheeling performance poetry designed to protest against social injustice, political hypocrisy and the nuclear threat. Since that sixties heyday Mitchell has continued to produce a poetry which is direct, fiercely committed to the individual's needs for freedom of all kinds and, perhaps most importantly, often very funny. He has also written novels and a number of plays including one based on the life and work of William Blake whom he has cited as his most important influence.

Blue Coffee: Poems 1895-1996
Bloodaxe pbk £8.95

Greeatest Hits
Bloodaxe pbk £5.95

Montague, John
(1929 -)

John Montague was born in New York but he grew up on his aunt's farm in County Tyrone and this rural upbringing has exercised a profound hold over his artistic imagination. He is regarded as the link between the poetic generation of Patrick Kavanagh and that of Seamus Heaney and Derek Mahon, who have expressed their admiration for his deeply felt lyrics and for his honest probing into the connections between Ulster's violent past and its troubled present. Montague has always shown an aversion to Yeatsian high rhetoric and his gaze on the workings of tribal politics and the realities of rural life has always been direct and straightforward. His most influential volume is *The Rough Field* (1972) which was described by Mahon as 'a rich and complex work by the best Irish poet of his generation.' *The Rough Field* was a multi-faceted meditation on Ulster's long history of oppressors and oppressed. An extraordinary stanzaic inventiveness, epigraphs and sidenotes, allied to an exciting mix of the historical and the autobiographical, of voices real and imagined, produced a dazzling tour de force. Montague edited *The Faber Book of Irish Verse* which included a number of his own verse translations and his *New Selected Poems* was published in 1990.

New Selected Poems
Bloodaxe pbk £5.95

The Rough Field
Bloodaxe pbk £5.95

Morgan, Edwin
(1920 -)

Born in Glasgow, Morgan was educated at the University there and went on to teach in the English department from 1947 until his retirement. His *Collected Poems* includes work from 1939 to 1988 and, as one critic has remarked, 'is unconfinable to any single mode.' Morgan plays with form and rhyme and has experimented with concrete and sound poetries. Much of his work is characterised by a sense of humour that is mischievous, surreal and unsettling.

Collected Poems
Carcanet pbk £14.95

Muir, Edwin
(1887 - 1959)

Muir was born in Orkney and spent his childhood there, an idyll devastatingly destroyed when the family moved to Glasgow and both parents and two of his brothers died in a short space of time. This personal expulsion from a perceived paradise is reflected in much of Muir's verse. The course of psychoanalysis which he undertook after moving to London to work as a freelance writer also affected his writing deeply and dreams and their significance recur throughout his work. His verse is traditional in form and technique and seemingly uninfluenced by contemporary modernism but, as T.S. Eliot observed, 'he found, almost unconsciously, the right, the inevitable way of saying the things he wanted to say.' He worked widely as a translator, most importantly of Kafka, and was the author of an evocative autobiography.

Collected Poems
Faber pbk £9.99

Muldoon, Paul
(1951 -)

Born in County Armagh, Muldoon was educated at Queen's University, Belfast where Seamus Heaney was amongst his lecturers. He has published nine collections of verse and has established a formidable reputation as one of the most inventive and unorthodox talents in poetry today. His 1994 collection, *The Annals of Chile,* was awarded the T.S. Eliot Prize that year. A useful and up-to-date introduction to Muldoon's work is his *New Selected Poems 1968 - 1994.* Presenting the poet's own selection from the nine collections and from *Shining Brow,* an opera libretto about Frank Lloyd Wright, this book charts his progression from the deceptive ease and clarity of his early collections to the weaving literary, historical and cultural allusions of *The Annals of Chile.* Described early in his career by Heaney as 'one of the very best' of contemporary writers, Muldoon has gone on to have significant influence on his generation of Irish poets.

The Annals of Chile
Faber pbk £8.99

New Selected Poems
Faber pbk £7.99

Nichols, Grace
(1950 -)

Grace Nichols was born and brought up in Guyana and has written a novel drawing on her Guyanese experience, *Whole of a Morning Sky*. She came to Britain in the seventies and has published several volumes of poetry which deal, in refreshingly unpompous and often comic form, with the experiences of black women in a white, male world and with everyday realities in contemporary Britain. The fat black woman of her best known collection is a brash celebrator of herself and the world around her and the poems have an engaging directness and wit.

**Lazy Thoughts
of a Lazy Woman**
Virago pbk £5.99

The Fat Black Woman's Poems
Virago pbk £5.99

Sunris
Virago pbk £7.99

O'Brien, Sean
(1952 -)

O'Brien grew up in Hull, was educated at Cambridge and Birmingham and, after periods of school and university teaching, now works as a freelance writer in Newcastle. His first collection was published in 1983 and, since then he has published three further volumes of his stylish, metrically inventive and socially committed poetry. His most recent book, *The Ghost Train*, published in 1995, displays the same interest in the textures of ordinary lives, the same anger at the malaise and complacency of eighties and nineties Britain as his previous volumes but shows a new subtlety and

The Lover (after Propertius)
by Don Paterson

Poor mortals, with your horoscopes and blood-tests -
what hope is there for you? Even if the plane
lands you safely, why should you not return
to your home in flames or ruins, your wife absconded,
the children blind and dying in their cots?
Even sitting quiet in a locked room
the perils are infinite and unforeseeable.
Only the lover walks upon the earth
careless of what the fates prepare for him:

so you step out at the lights, almost as if
you half-know that today you are the special one.
The woman in the windshield lifting away
her frozen cry, a white mask on a stick,
reveals herself as grey-eyed Atropos;
the sun leaves like a rocket; the sky goes out;
the road floods and widens; on the distant kerb
the lost souls call to you like sad trombones;
the ambulance glides up with its black sail -

when somewhere in the other world, she fills
your name full of her breath again, and at once
you float to your feet: the dark rose on your shirt
folds itself away, and you slip back
into the crowd, who, being merely human,
must remember nothing of this incident.
Just one flea-ridden dog chained to the railings,
who might be Cerberus, or patient Argos,
looks on, knowing the great law you have flouted.

sophistication in his interminglings of history, politics and autobiography.

Ghost Train
Oxford UP pbk £6.99

Owen, Wilfred
(1893 - 1918)

Owen is now remembered as the greatest of the World War I poets, although only a handful of his poems were published before his death in France a mere week before the armistice. The edition of his poems produced in 1931 by Edmund Blunden, together with a memoir, established his reputation as the creator of richly elegiac evocations of the horror and the pity of the war. His imaginative range and his high technical skills marked him out as a poet even more gifted than his mentor Sassoon.

Poems
Chatto pbk £5.99

War Poems of Wilfred Owen
Chatto pbk £4.99

Paterson, Don
(1963 -)

Born in Dundee, Paterson came to the fore with his collection *Nil Nil*, published in 1993, and he was selected as one of the New Generation poets of 1994. His second collection *God's Gift to Women* is due from Faber in 1997. *Nil Nil* is an impressive and unsettling collection in which imagery from a Scottish working class landscape, philosophical diversions and

surreal, imaginative excursions are equally present. A down-to-earth sensibility is frequently undercut by playful demonstrations of the artifice of poetry and by the games Paterson plays with readers' expectations. The characteristic density of Paterson's work, especially in longer poems, and his technical expertise set him apart as one of the most intelligent and original voices to emerge in recent years.

Nil Nil
Faber pbk £6.99

Patten, Brian
(1946 -)

The youngest of the Liverpool poets, Patten was in his early twenties when the bestselling volume of his work, together with that of McGough and Henri, appeared in the Penguin Modern Poets series. Like his fellow Liverpudlians he was committed, and has remained so, to the idea of poetry as performance, accessible and immediate. He has continued to publish regular collections of observational, comic and love lyrics which have retained their popularity. He has also published a number of successful books of children's poetry.

Armada
HarperCollins pbk £5.99

Love Poems
HarperCollins pbk £4.99

Storm Damage
HarperCollins pbk £5.99

Tom Paulin

Paulin, Tom
(1949 -)

Paulin, a lecturer in English at Nottingham University, is an astringent critic, essayist and polemicist in books, newspapers and, more recently, on television. His own beliefs in the importance of a literature rooted in the realities of politics and history and his disdain for the view that poets possess 'an ability to hold themselves above history rather like a skylark or a weather satellite' are bracing antidotes to sentimentality and complacent thought. His own poetry represents an increasingly imaginative and various attempt to grapple with political and cultural realities particularly in the Northern Ireland where he grew up.

Selected Poems 1972 - 1990
Faber pbk £5.99

Walking a Line
Faber pbk £6.99

Pierpoint, Katherine
(1961 -)

Katherine Pierpoint was born in Northampton, read languages at Exeter University and, after a period working in publishing, is now a freelance writer living in London. Her first collection *Truffle Beds*, published in 1995, won immediate acclaim for its rich use of language, the acute visual sense it displayed and its compelling inventiveness.

Truffle Beds
Faber pbk £6.99

Katherine Pierpoint

Porter, Peter
(1929 -)

Born in Australia, Porter came to Britain as a young man and has lived here since. His early verse, published in the fifties and sixties, was satiric and ironic, the work of an outsider recording with detached fascination the society into which he had come. Since his debut he has been a prolific writer whose poetry has matured impressively to accommodate a far-ranging allusiveness to the European culture in which he has steeped himself, the stoical and compassionate acceptance of suffering and transience and an interest in dreams and the transformative power of language.

Collected Poems
Oxford UP pbk £7.99

Millennial Fables
Oxford UP pbk £7.99

Raine, Craig
(1944 -)

Raine was educated at Oxford and his career since has been divided between academic life and the world of publishing - he was poetry editor at Faber for ten years - and reviewing. His second collection, *A Martian Sends A Postcard Home,* was much acclaimed and gave its name to a particular, 'Martian', school of writing in which startling similes and metaphors are used to revitalise language and create the world afresh, as if seen by alien eyes. In fact the originality of the Martian approach to poetry can be exaggerated. The effects Raine was creating, and has continued to create in later collections, are those of much good poetry - renewing the world for the reader by the use of fresh and re-animating language.

Clay: Whereabouts Unknown
Penguin pbk £7.99

**A Martian Sends
A Postcard Home**
Oxford UP pbk £6.99

Reading, Peter
(1946 -)

Reading, 'the unofficial laureate of a decaying England' as Tom Paulin has described him, has spent a quarter of a century creating a body of work that marks him out as one of the most original and challenging of contemporary poets. His skilful use of direct and uncompromising language within highly developed metrical and syllabic patterns to produce his bitter, satirical accounts of blighted lives and of a country steeped in hypocrisy, mean-spiritedness and the degraded language of the tabloid press, is highly distinctive and his voice unmistakable.

Collected Poems 1
Bloodaxe pbk £9.95

Collected Poems 2
Bloodaxe pbk £9.95

Redgrove, Peter
(1932 -)

Redgrove studied science at Cambridge and was a founder member of the Group, the informal association of writers that grew up in the mid-fifties. His poetry has been an interesting fusion of the observational precision engendered by his scientific training with a profoundly mystical sense of the forces operating within the natural world and within the individual. He has drawn on the imagery of dreams, his wide reading in Jungian and other psychologies and a knowledge of mythologies to produce a poetry that has been described as 'most likely to surprise us with a quality of pure inspiration.' In partnership with his wife, the poet and novelist Penelope Shuttle, he has also written several novels and *The Wise Wound,* a striking examination of menstruation and the myths surrounding it.

My Father's Trap Door
Cape pbk £7.00

Reid, Christopher
(1949 -)

Christopher Reid, currently poetry editor at Faber, has published five collections of his poems, the most recent entitled *Expanded Universes,* and has received a Somerset Maugham Award and Hawthornden Prize for his work. Reid's third and best-known volume builds on his interest in character and parody, presenting a selection from the work of a fictional female East European poet Katerina Brac. Skilfully mimicking the style and intonations characteristic of translation, Reid enters so fully the voice of Brac that these half-serious variations on serious themes transcend the deceit on which they are based.

Expanded Universes
Faber pbk £6.99

Katerina Brac
Faber pbk £4.99

Rosenberg, Isaac
(1890 - 1918)

Rosenberg's poor, urban Jewish background - he was brought up in the East End - gives his poems a gritty and direct quality not found in the work of his fellow war poets. Although he had published poetry before the war he was almost unknown at the time of his death in action and it was only the publication of his *Collected Works* in 1937 that established his posthumous reputation. Rosenberg hated what he described as the 'begloried sonnets' of Rupert Brooke and his best poetry is characterised by an angrily unsentimental realism, often set within very loose metrical forms.

Collected Works
Chatto pbk £12.95

Rumens, Carol
(1944 -)

From her first collection Rumens has shown an awareness of that necessary integration of the personal and the political, the individual's relationships and the larger social context in which they are played out. Her refreshingly direct verse has moved from sharply focused portraits of domestic life to darker and more complex poems dealing with exile, political persecution and the legacy of the Holocaust. Many of the poems in her most recent collection, *Best China Sky*, were written in Northern Ireland where she worked at Queen's University, Belfast and owe much to her response to events in the province. The collection also includes reworkings of Celtic fables, poems about growing up in postwar London and translations from Russian.

Best China Sky
Bloodaxe pbk £6.95

Thinking of Skins
Bloodaxe pbk £8.95

Sassoon, Siegfried
(1886 - 1967)

Sassoon was on service in Flanders throughout much of the First World War and his poems, filled with compassion for his fellow-soldiers and an angry contempt for the generals and for the patriotic cant of wartime, were amongst the first recognitions of the realities of that conflict. His first collection was published in 1917, the same year in which he threw away the Military Cross he had been awarded for conspicuous bravery and launched his own one-man campaign against the conduct of the war. Sent to hospital, allegedly suffering from shell-shock, he met Wilfred Owen and gave much encouragement to the younger man's poetry. Sassoon continued to write and publish poetry after the war, much of it concerned with the religious and spiritual development which eventually led him into the Catholic church. He also published a semi-autobiographical trilogy *The Complete Memoirs of George Sherston* and several volumes of more openly autobiographical writings.

Collected Poems
Faber pbk £12.99

War Poems of Siegfried Sassoon
Faber pbk £6.99

Shuttle, Penelope
(1947 -)

Penelope Shuttle is married to fellow poet Peter Redgrove and her work in a number of different forms – novels, radio plays, pre-eminently poetry – covers the same terrain as his, although from a complementary, feminine viewpoint. Dreams are important, so too are the tribal and national dreams known as mythology. Ritual is significant as a means of entering areas of mystery and elusiveness otherwise closed to the rigidly realistic mind. Her poetry is funny, surreal, constantly inventive and has a powerful cumulative effect.

Building a City for Jamie
Oxford UP pbk £7.99

Smith, Iain Crichton
(1928 -)

Born in Glasgow Iain Crichton Smith was brought up on the island of Lewis. At home he spoke Gaelic and at school English. This bilingual inheritance has remained a central preoccupation in his poetry and he has been prolific in both languages. For forty years he has delineated and discussed the hard life of the rural communities he knows so well and deplored the steady erosion of the Gaelic language and culture. Much of his work is traditional in that it is iambic and rhymed although in his later volumes he has developed a facility for a freer line and rhythm. He has never been happy to write in a particular voice or mode for very long and his considerable body of work encompasses a great variety of influences and forms. Despite receiving many awards he remains, outside Scotland, an unfashionable poet although in England Michael Schmidt's Carcanet Press has consistently celebrated his work, publishing both his poetry and prose. His *Collected Poems* was published in 1992.

Collected Poems
Carcanet hbk £25.00

Selected Poems
Carcanet pbk £6.95

Smith, Ken
(1938 -)

Smith, who was born in Yorkshire and educated at Leeds University, is one of England's most interesting contemporary poets and has been described by one critic as 'irreplaceable....truth-teller to a meretricious age'. His early work shared the social commitment of other poets associated, as he was, with the magazine *Stand* and his later volumes have seen his poetry developing in response to the different environments in England and America in which

he has lived and worked. Perhaps most memorable is his representation of the hostile urban landscape of London in the long poem *Fox Running*, included in *The Poet Reclining*, a selection of his poetry from 1962 - 1980, although *Wormwood*, poems written while he was writer-in-residence at Wormwood Scrubs and working with lifers and others confined both physically and mentally, is notable for its skill and insight.

The Poet Reclining: Selected Poems 1962 -1980
Bloodaxe pbk £7.95

Wormwood
Bloodaxe pbk £4.95

Smith, Stevie
(1902 - 1971)

Born in Hull but brought up in the North London suburb of Palmers Green where she continued to live for most of the rest of her life, Stevie Smith was a highly idiosyncratic poet. Her work ranges in tone from the whimsical to the caustic, from the theologically serious to the self-consciously absurd. In technique, too, she was *sui generis*, an inspired improviser in a wide variety of forms and an effective exponent of 'free verse'. Her collections were often illustrated by her own eccentric sketches.

Selected Poems
Penguin pbk £6.99

Stevie Smith : A Selection
Faber pbk £8.99

Spender, Stephen
(1909 - 1995)

Spender's death last year removed the last important link with the Auden generation of thirties poets. Indeed it was Spender's poem *The Pylons*, collected in one of his first volumes that gave the alternative name 'the Pylon poets' to that group of young left-wing poets, alluding to their occasionally self-conscious use of industrial imagery. Much of Spender's best known verse was written in this period but, in common with his friends, he moved away from a direct commitment to doctrinaire socialism and his work during and after the war emphasised the lyric and the personal which had always hovered beneath the surface of his thirties poetry. His autobiography *World Within World*, first published in the early fifties, is an important book for the understanding of the intellectual history of his generation.

Collected Poems
Faber pbk £8.99

Szirtes, George
(1948 -)

Szirtes was born in Hungary but came to England with his parents following the 1956 uprising. He studied Fine Art at Leeds and began to exhibit his painting and publish his poetry at the same time. His work, since the publication of his first volume in 1980, has met with great critical acclaim. His poetry has often been concerned with the darker European past and the past of his own family - Metro, for example, is a long poem set in Hungary in 1944-5 when fascist forces came to power - but he has also published poems about more contemporary events which share a similar interest in the intermingling of private and public, the fate of individual lives caught up in large events. His *Selected Poems*, drawing on a number of volumes, was published in 1996.

Selected Poems
Oxford UP pbk £9.99

Thomas, Dylan
(1914 - 1953)

Born in Swansea, Thomas began to write poetry as a schoolboy and his first volume was published in 1934, the year of his move to London and his embarkation on a precarious career as freelance writer and broadcaster. In literary London he rapidly established his reputation for flamboyant behaviour and heavy drinking. His volumes after the war extended his popularity as a poet, leading to invitations to reading tours of the States, on one of which he succumbed, still in his thirties, to a lethal combination of drink and drugs taken to combat exhaustion. The legend of Dylan Thomas - the doomed and drunken bard declaiming his wild and rhetorical verse - was strong in his lifetime and has survived the forty years since his death. In most ways the legend serves to emphasise the worst aspects of Thomas' poetry, its occasional formlessness and repetitiousness, and to obscure his commitment to his craft and the genuine beauties and originality of his writing. Poems such as *Fern Hill, Do not go gentle into that good night, Poem in October* and *In my craft and sullen art* are poems as good as all but the greatest produced this century.

Collected Poems 1934 - 1953
Dent pbk £4.99

Notebook Poems 1930 - 1934
Dent pbk £4.99

Selected Poems
Dent pbk £3.99

Thomas, Edward
(1878 - 1917)

In the first years of the century Thomas supported himself and his family by producing a long series of prose works, mainly topographical and biographical, and he began to write poetry only in 1914, largely at the instigation of his close friend Robert Frost. Between then and his death in the First World War he continued to write verse although little of it was published. Posthumous collections and the support of Frost and other early enthusiasts, including (perhaps surprisingly) F. R. Leavis, helped to establish his reputation. Thomas' verse transcends the sentimental nostalgia of other 'Georgian' poets, whom he resembles superficially, largely because his skill in evoking and celebrating the life of the countryside is subtly entwined with a clear-eyed acknowledgement of the ways in which it was changing around him.

Collected Poems
Faber pbk £7.99

Selected Poems
Faber pbk £6.99

Thomas, R. S.
(1913 -)

Thomas was a parish priest in remote Welsh villages for more than forty years and his poetry, particularly in his earlier collections, reflects his experience of the harsh, unforgiving landscape in which his parishioners eked out cramped and confined lives. His compassion for the unfulfilled is matched by his anger at the social conditions which have shaped their lives and for the marginalisation of Wales and the Welsh language. He has been an outspoken and opinionated voice in the nationalist movement and in the campaign to restore the Welsh language to its rightful place. He has also produced what can be seen as the most sustained body of religious poetry this century, a poetry which reveals the doubts that lie behind faith but which finally attains a hard-won affirmation.

Collected Poems
Phoenix pbk £9.99

No Truce with the Furies
Bloodaxe pbk £7.95

Selected Poems 1946-68
Bloodaxe pbk £7.95

Thwaite, Anthony
(1930 -)

Thwaite's career has been divided between academic life in this country and abroad and periods as literary editor of publications such as *The Listener* and *The New Statesman*. His early poetry, much influenced by Larkin whose *Collected Poems* he edited, is urbane, commonsensical and accessible. Later his historical interests and an interest in other cultures, not an interest notably shared by Larkin, led him into more adventurous work and a discovered skill in dramatic monologue was put to interesting effect in *Victorian Voices*, in which he adopts the voices of a number of minor Victorian cultural figures.

Dust in the World
Sinclair Stevenson pbk £6.99

Tomlinson, Charles
(1927 -)

Tomlinson was educated at Cambridge where he was taught by, among others, Donald Davie and has pursued a career as an academic. He has taught at the University of Bristol since 1957 and has been professor of English literature there since 1982. In his own poetry, published since the fifties, he has reacted against what he sees as the insularity and complacency of much of contemporary English poetry and his influences have always been strongly American - Stevens and William Carlos Williams, for example - or European, drawing on his work as a translator. Yet he remains very much an English poet in his strongly visual responses to landscapes and experiences - he is also a graphic artist of considerable skill - and in his sense of the otherness of the observable world. ' In both graphic and poetic art,' he has written, 'I like something lucid surrounded by something mysterious' and the comment could be applied to many of his own poems.

Jubilation
Oxford UP pbk £6.99

Williams, Hugo
(1942 -)

Williams was associated with the literary magazines *The Review* and its successor *The New Review* and his early poetry reflected the pared-down minimalism that was characteristic of the work of many contributors and of the editor, Ian Hamilton. Devoid of rhetoric, his work was restrained, intense and resonant. In his later collections he has moved towards a greater freedom and a more relaxed style in which he has been able to consider more personal subject matter such as his relationship with his actor father, Hugh Williams.

Selected Poems
Oxford UP pbk £7.95

An Irish Airman Foresees his Death
by W.B. Yeats

I know that I shall meet my fate
Somewhere among the clouds above;
Those that I fight I do not hate,
Those that I guard I do not love;
My country is Kiltartan Cross,
My countrymen Kiltartan's poor,
No likely end could bring them loss
Or leave them happier than before.
Nor law, nor duty bade me fight
Nor public men, nor cheering crowds,
A lonely impulse of delight
Drove to this tumult in the clouds;
I balanced all, brought all to mind,
The years to come seemed waste of breath
A waste of breath the years behind
In balance with this life, this death.

Yeats, W. B.
(1865 - 1939)

Yeats was born in Dublin - his father was the Irish artist John Butler Yeats - and his early life was divided between Ireland and London. His first book of verse appeared in 1889 and drew heavily on the Irish mythology and traditions which were soon to be such important components of the Irish literary revival of the nineties and early nineteen hundreds. His early verse also shows the heavy influence of Yeats' interest in mysticism and the occult - he was a member of many of the esoteric societies that flourished in the period - and of his long, largely unrequited love for the actress and Irish nationalist Maud Gonne. Through her Yeats was also led to his productive involvement, both as playwright and as co-director of the Abbey Theatre, with the Irish stage. The tragedy of the Easter Rising and the tumult of the ensuing years affected Yeats deeply and he became an increasingly public figure - he was a senator in the Irish Free State for six years in the twenties. His private life in this period was shaped by his late marriage and by the mediumistic powers his new wife apparently possessed. Her automatic writing was instrumental in the creation of Yeats' philosophical credo *A Vision*, published in 1925 and, indirectly, the flowering of his late poetry. Yeats died in France in 1939 and was the subject of a great elegy by Auden. Yeats was, indisputably, the greatest Irish poet of the century and the remarkable development of his verse from its lush *fin de siècle* beginnings to the spare power of his later verse, the single-minded construction of his own private symbolism - the rose, the dancer, the tower and the star are all of recurring importance - and the capacity to speak through many diverse voices - his 'masks' as Yeats referred to them - are all of enduring interest and influence.

Collected Poems
Vintage pbk £8.99

Collected Poems
Pan pbk £9.99

Selected Poems
Pan pbk £5.99

Zephaniah, Benjamin
(1958 -)

Born in Birmingham and brought up in Jamaica and Handsworth, Zephaniah ended a troubled adolescence with a jail sentence for burglary. Turning from crime to poetry and music, he has become a superb exponent of performance poetry and one of the significant voices of the Afro-Caribbean experience in Britain, fiercely and wittily resistant to marginalisation and suppression. As well as books of his poetry, he has produced children's poetry, released several records and in 1989 was a popular candidate for Professor of Poetry at Oxford.

Propa Propaganda
Bloodaxe pbk £6.95

White Comedy
by Benjamin Zephaniah

I waz whitemailed
By a white witch,
Wid white magic
An white lies,
Branded a white sheep
I slaved as a whitesmith
Near a white spot
Where I suffered whitewater fever.
Whitelisted as a whiteleg
I waz in de white book
As a master of de white art,
It waz like white death.

People called me white jack
Some hailed me as white wog,
So I joined de white watch
Trained as a white guard
Lived off de white economy.
Caught an beaten by de whiteshirts
I waz condemned to a white mass.

Don't worry,
I shall be writing to de Black House.

Commonwealth Poetry

Atwood, Margaret
(1939 -)

Atwood, one of Canada's most distinguished writers, is best known for novels such as *The Edible Woman* and *The Handmaid's Tale* but she has written poetry throughout her career and published her first collection in the mid-sixties. Her poetry covers the same terrain as her fiction - the politics of gender, the difficulties of love, the distracting power of memory - in a distinctive idiom in which the mundane and the bizarre are imaginatively intermingled. Her most recent collection includes both poetic fantasies in which Helen of Troy appears as a tabletop dancer and Cressida enlightens us as to her real feelings about Troilus and moving meditations about the death of a parent.

Poems 1976 - 1986
Virago pbk £7.99

Morning in the Burned House
Virago pbk £8.99

Baxter, James K.
(1926 - 1972)

Baxter, one of New Zealand's finest poets, published his first volume when he was only eighteen and he was conspicuously prolific throughout a career that was cut short by his early death at the age of 46. His sense of the poet's necessary isolation from the society in which he works, the religious convictions and experiences which led to his conversion to Catholicism, his contempt for what he saw as the shoddy meretriciousness of much of contemporary culture and his powerful responses to the landscape and people of New Zealand all emerge clearly from the work in his *Collected Poems*.

Collected Poems
Oxford UP pbk £17.50

Edmond, Lauris
(1924 -)

One of New Zealand's most distinguished poets, Lauris Edmond did not publish her first collection until she was in her fifties but has since produced regular volumes of her warm and direct poetry. She deals with the themes of the everyday – love, family relationships, the losses and griefs of ordinary lives – but she invests them with a particular observation and attention to language which raises them above the everyday. Her mature voice – resilient and affirmative yet aware of loss and the fragility of the present as time passes – is apparent in her new collection.

In Position
Bloodaxe pbk £6.95

New and Selected Poems
pbk £7.95

Hope, A.D.
(1907 -)

One of the most prominent and influential of all Australian poets, A.D. Hope, although he wrote poetry from an early age, did not publish his first collection until 1955, when his satiric, erotic and erudite verse had an immediate impact. His poetry, often concerned with conflict between man and nature and conflict between the sexes, is characterised by a tension between his sense of abundance and his sense of aridity. He is caught between fierce passions and an equally fierce, sceptical wit, between the high seriousness he demands of poetry and a sardonic impatience with human folly. Although variously accused over the years of crimes against political correctness, Hope's work is central to Australian poetry this century.

Selected Poems
Carcanet pbk £5.95

Murray, Les A.
(1938 -)

Murray was brought up on a dairy farm in New South Wales, a homeland to which he returned in the eighties after long residence in Sydney. Many of his poems evoke that community, his 'spirit country' as he has called it, its landscapes and its values. From the perspective of that spirit-country the idiocies of life in Sydney have seemed striking and Murray has written much witty and satirical verse surveying the urban scene with varying degrees of geniality. An increasing interest in narrative, in the telling of stories, has been apparent in his work since the late seventies and one of his most ambitious works is the novel in verse *The Boys Who Stole the Funeral*, in which the tale of two boys stealing the body of an old man to return it to the country where he wished to be buried is freighted with allusions to Murray's own Roman Catholic beliefs.

Selected Poems
Carcanet pbk £6.95

Les Murray

Seth, Vikram
(1952 -)

Seth's epic novel *A Suitable Boy* has been one of publishing's great success stories in the past few years. Before the publication of *A Suitable Boy,* he was best known as a poet although he has also written a book about his travels in China. The graceful and elegant verses in his collection *The Humble Administrator's Garden* often reflect encounters with cultures, both Eastern and Western, very different to his own background in Calcutta. *The Golden Gate* was a remarkably ambitious attempt to create a novel in verse, telling the stories of a group of affluent Californians, using the same stanzaic form used by Pushkin in *Eugene Onegin.*

The Golden Gate
Faber pbk £6.99

The Humble Administrator's Garden
Carcanet pbk £6.95

Wright, Judith
(1915 -)

The *grande dame* of Australian poetry has published many volumes of her energetic and skilful verse since her first volume appeared in 1946. She has been described as a 'nature' poet and certainly much of her writing springs from her feelings for the landscape, environment and people of Australia - she has also been a notable campaigner for conservation and the protection of wildlife - but the description is an inadequate one. As she herself has written, 'Anything I have ever written has had its human meaning even if it started from the natural.'

A Human Pattern: Selected Poems
Carcanet hbk £14.95

Walcott, Derek
(1930 -)

Although his first collection was published before he was twenty, it was probably not until the publication of the autobiographical *Another Life* in 1973 that Walcott reached a wide readership. His *Collected Poems* appeared in 1987. Through his long career Walcott has wrestled with the dual heritage of a local culture and an overlaid colonial culture. From Caribbean registers and constructions via the long tradition of literary English he has forged a vibrant poetic lexicon creating 'where nothing was/ the language of a race.' Rich in learning, sensual and approachable, his work has been preoccupied with the accumulated identities of the West Indies, which has subsumed Africa, European and Indian influences. His long-time fascination with Homer's Odyssey was triumphantly realised in his most ambitious work the book-length *Omeros* (1989). Here, re-employing Homer's characters in a contemporary setting and with narrative clarity, he uncovered the tragic history of the Caribbean. *Omeros* was received as a masterpiece and in 1992 Walcott was awarded the Nobel Prize.

Collected Poems 1948-84
Faber pbk £9.95

Omeros
Faber pbk £9.99

photo Nigel Parry

Portrait of Derek Walcott

American Verse

Angelou, Maya
(1928 -)

Maya Angelou is amongst the most successful and celebrated of African-American writers. She is best known for her series of prose autobiographical works, beginning with *I Know Why The Caged Bird Sings,* but is also an esteemed poet who has produced several volumes of poetry, largely portraying strong African-American characters with witty, intelligent language and a confident sense of rhythm and form. Her standing as a major American writer was confirmed in 1993 when she was invited to read her poem *Pulse of Morning* at President Clinton's inauguration service.

Complete Collected Poems
Virago pbk £9.99

Ashbery, John
(1927 -)

It is now commonplace for John Ashbery, who published his first collection in 1953, to be acclaimed as the most influential or the most important of his generation. Approaching his seventieth year he has gained innumerable awards including the Pulitzer Prize for *Self Portrait in a Convex Mirror* (1976). His work is relentlessly playful and witty, but also teasingly difficult and, at times, wholly impenetrable as his experimental poetic world is uncompromisingly interiorised. To the fey, inconsequential stance of the New York School with which he was originally associated he added the obliquities and found poetry of the French surrealist poets he continues to admire. His elliptical, entertaining lyrics and expansive meditations are instantly recognisable, a generous humour masking a bracing intellectual toughness. The themes he addresses consistently are those of the modern French and Francophile literary theorists: the relationship between art and life and the inadmissibility of a coherent and uniform personality, viewpoint or narrative - 'standing there helplessly/ While the poem streaked by, its tail afire, a bad/ Comet screaming hate and disaster, but so turned inward/ That the meaning, good or other, can never / Become known.'

Can You Hear, Bird
Carcanet pbk £9.95

And the Stars Were Shining
Carcanet pbk £8.95

Self-Portrait in a Convex Mirror
Carcanet pbk £6.95

Berryman, John
(1914 - 1972)

Berryman's life was a difficult one, disordered by a long addiction to drink, and was ended by a leap from a bridge over the Mississippi. He saw the turbulence of this life given shape by his poetry, although by the time of the publication of his most famous work, *The Dream Songs* in 1969, even this belief in redemption through art was beginning to look slightly threadbare. *The Dream Songs,* like much of his work, were anguished and confessional although shaped by his technical skill and enlivened by his wit and erudition.

The Dream Songs
Faber pbk £9.99

Selected Poems
Faber pbk £6.99

Bishop, Elizabeth
(1911-1979)

Born and raised in New England, Bishop travelled widely, before settling in Brazil, where, in addition to writing much of her own poetry, she also translated the work of leading Brazilian poets, including Carlos Drummond de Andrade. Bishop was something of a poet's poet. Her talent was appreciated and encouraged early on by Marianne Moore, with whom she shared a perfectionist streak in reworking and honing her poems. Throughout her output, which has tremendous thematic range, there is a controlled subtlety and understatement, both in perception and expression, which gives depth and resonance to her poems. Robert Lowell put it well when he said 'She has a humorous, commanding genius for picking up the unnoticed, now making something sprightly and right, and now for the great monument.'

Complete Poems
Chatto pbk £10.99

Bukowski, Charles
(1920 - 1994)

Bukowski lived most of his life in and around Los Angeles and his poetry, indebted to the Beats, is a poetry of the seedy and sleazy side of urban life - of drinking too much in run-down bars, of walking mean streets and of one-night stands in dirty flophouses. His work can be seen as a further development of the lasting trend in American poetry against the formal and the intellectual and has won a considerable readership amongst people not generally interested in contemporary poetry. Although not as artless as it first appears, Bukowski's poetry depends largely on the direct impact of the authorial voice - colloquial, uninhibited and often very funny.

Betting on the Muse: Poems and Stories
Black Sparrow Press pbk £12.99

Burning in Water, Drowning in Flame
Black Sparrow Press pbk £7.95

Love is a Dog From Hell
Black Sparrow Press pbk £12.99

Carver, Raymond
(1939 - 1988)

Noted primarily for his short stories, stark and unembellished accounts of American blue collar life, Carver also wrote several volumes of poetry. This shares with his fiction a consciously flat diction and a refusal of any linguistic flamboyance but concentrates on material drawn from Carver's own life history - his alcoholism, his late discovery of enduring love with fellow poet Tess Gallagher and his brave battles with cancer.

All of Us: Collected Poems
Harvill hbk £20.00

A New Path to the Waterfall
Harvill pbk £8.95

Corso, Gregory
(1930 -)

Corso was one of the earliest of the Beat writers and it can be argued that he has clung to the battered ideals of that generation more tenaciously than any of the other survivors. He spent three years in prison as a very young man, published his first collection in 1955, was befriended by Ginsberg and Kerouac and has continued to publish collections of verse even during times when his work has gone more or less unnoticed. His work, in common with that of other Beats, values spontaneity and a child-like openness to experience above any formal considerations.

Gasoline and Vestal Lady on Brattle
City Lights pbk £6.95

Crane, Hart
(1899 - 1932)

In his relatively brief career, ended when, troubled by increasing dependence on alcohol and confusions about his sexuality, he jumped from a boat bringing him back from Mexico to New York, Hart Crane produced a body of work that has met with much critical acclaim. His best known poem is *The Bridge,* a massive work of American modernism which, ironically in view of Crane's own end, is an attempt to present an optimistic and affirmative vision of America and its history, held in place by the central image of the Brooklyn Bridge.

The Bridge
Liveright pbk £7.00

Creeley, Robert
(1926 -)

Creeley belongs to a long tradition of American poets, whose poetic voice is highly personal, to the point of being idiosyncratic. In Creeley's case, his short, ametrical poems are sometimes reminiscent of Emily Dickinson, especially as part of the impact of his work rests in the concentration achieved by his use of line and ellipsis. However, unlike Dickinson, Creeley was heavily involved in the literary world, both as a teacher at Black Mountain College and subsequent editor of the Black Mountain Review.

Collected Poems
University of California Press pbk £12.95

e.e. cummings
(1894 - 1962)

On account of his syntactical innovations, his rejection of capital letters and his habit of utilising typography as a deliberate visual element in his poetry, it is easy to label cummings as an innovator, even as a member of the avant garde. However, rather like the Mersey poets, cummings was something of a populariser, writing poems that were generally accessible and addressing many conventional themes. Indeed, something of his essential conservatism can be seen in the way in which he did not move on stylistically or in his range of subjects throughout his forty year career. Nevertheless, cummings did pave the way for many later poets, including the Beats, with his unusual, highly idiosyncratic approach to composition and expression.

Selected Poems 1923-1958
Faber pbk £6.99

Dickinson, Emily
(1830 - 1886)

Outwardly an extremely private and virtually reclusive indi-vidual, who secluded herself throughout her life in her native town of Amherst, Massachussetts, Emily Dickinson was possessed of an inner life that was a torrent of passionate sensitivities, which found expression in her poetry. Her poems are startlingly unique, betraying almost no obvious influences, and are mostly exquisite miniatures of compressed imagery, written in halting rhythms and cadences. The most obvious visual signature of her poems is her use of dashes as the dominant method of punctuation, a technique which contributes to the sensation of ellipsis and depth which her poems convey. The fact that most of her prodigious output of nearly 1000 lyrics was achieved in a brief six year period in the 1860s and that all but a handful remained unpublished in her lifetime only add to the intrigue that surrounds this remarkable figure in American literary history.

A Choice of Emily Dickinson's Verse (ed Ted Hughes)
Faber pbk £5.99

Complete Poems
Faber pbk £13.99

Dobyns, Stephen
(1941 -)

Dobyns is a poet and crime writer, author of the Charlie Bradshaw detective novels, and possessor of the, perhaps, ambivalent distinction of being the favourite poet of horror writer Stephen King who has quoted Dobyns' poetry in his fiction. Dobyns characteristically creates strange narratives, weaving dark fables of a world simultaneously recognisable and unrecognisable as the one in which we live our lives. His poems are often frightening, sometimes very funny and invite the reader, as one critic noted, 'to see the fantastic as routine, as one does in Kafka.' *Velocities*, published in 1996, is a selection which draws on all his collections so far. A new collection, *Common Carnage*, is due from Bloodaxe in 1997.

Velocities:
New and Selected Poems
Bloodaxe pbk £10.95

Widened Horizons
by Stephen Dobyns

A big ant hauls a small ant up a stick.
Do we call this fellowship or lunch? Let's say
the short guy mangled his paw on a tack
and his pal provides a kindly lift. Let's say

the shrimp has contracted a terminal ailment
and his buddy carts him everywhere tout de suite.
Back in real life the big ant lugs the small ant
into an ant restaurant. I brought my own steak,

he says. Make sure you cook it right! How cynical!
comes the anticipated complaint. But how quaint
is our human perspective. Isn't it possible

that all three fabrications are correct? Can't
we envy a full life cracking ant jokes and when
we die we're served as supper for our friends?

Doolittle, Hilda (H. D.)
(1886 - 1961)

H.D. is best known for her early work when, in the company of Pound and others, she was one of the Imagist group. Indeed, she was the quintessential Imagist, composing short, intense, concentrated poems, including the extraordinary *Oread*, arguably the definitive Imagist poem. In 1913, she married Richard Aldington and moved to England, and increasingly her work from this point moves on from the early Imagist phase, partly due to a natural growth in the scope and ambition of her ideas, and partly because the psychological anguish she suffered (not helped by Aldington's infidelities) meant that her work could not be contained within such a tight framework. By the end of her life, H.D. had a large and impressive body of work, which included translations from Greek, novels and the magnificent epic *Helen in Egypt* which was posthumously published in 1961. Often neglected during her life, her reputation is now assured as one of the most important American poets of the twentieth century.

Selected Poems
Carcanet pbk £14.95

Doty, Mark

Mark Doty's third collection, *My Alexandria,* was his first to be published in Britain. When it appeared in 1995 it was greeted with huge enthusiasm as the product of a poet fit to extend the tradition of Wallace Stevens and Robert Lowell. Doty was lauded for his extraordinary technical virtuosity, for the tactile beauty of his language and for the directness of his description of gay relationships. *Atlantis* (1996), his latest volume, displays the same assured technical skills as well as an astounding maturity and courage. The collection inhabits a world disfigured by the poet's loss of his lover to AIDS (Doty has also written a prose memoir of his bereavement, *Heaven's Boast*) in which movingly he continues to find opportunities for affirmation.

Atlantis
Cape pbk £7.00

My Alexandria
Cape pbk £7.00

Ferlinghetti, Lawrence
(1919 -)

Long resident in San Francisco, Ferlinghetti was the owner of the City Lights bookshop, the publisher of Ginsberg's *Howl*, a central text of the fifties, and one of the leading figures in the Beat generation. His own poetry, particularly the bestselling *A Coney Island of the Mind*, has the spontaneity, passion and immediacy associated with the best of the verse produced by the Beats. He has continued to produce collections regularly and his more recent verse can still be sharp and funny, although the directness and colloquial language which seemed so refreshing in the fifties have been overtaken by cultural developments of the last thirty years.

A Coney Island of the Mind
City Lights pbk £6.95

Frost, Robert
(1874 - 1963)

The most 'English' of poets, Frost would surely have become Poet Laureate were it not for the geographical hiccup of having been born in San Francisco. Having moved to New Hampshire as a child, Frost went on to study at Harvard and become a farmer, an experience which provided him with the bulk of his material throughout life. He published relatively little poetry until he sold his farm

Gallagher, Tess
(1932-)

Tess Gallagher's third husband was the poet and short-story writer Raymond Carver and many of the most moving poems in her collection *My Black Horse: New and Selected Poems* are those which she wrote in mourning and remembrance after his early death from cancer in 1988. Her most recent collection in this country, *Portable Kisses*, began life as a hand-printed limited edition in 1978 but has continued to grow and further poems have been added in the years since. An entire book of poems, both playful and serious, devoted to the kiss is something to celebrate and, as Tess Gallagher has herself said, 'Ideally, a reader should finish this book, then find someone to kiss.'

My Black Horse: New and Selected Poems
Bloodaxe pbk £8.95

Portable Kisses
Bloodaxe pbk £7.95

Ginsberg, Allen
(1926 -)

The most famous of the Beat poets, Ginsberg is still best-known for his fifties poem *Howl;* with its driving, colloquial beat and its drop-out romanticism, it represents the rhetorical voice of the popular American tradition, a tradition best exemplified by Whitman to whom Ginsberg is obviously indebted. His

and moved to England for three years, during which time he befriended Edward Thomas and encouraged him on his literary career. On his return to New Hampshire, Frost's own career took off, and he became known for his well-crafted nature poems. The judgement of history has not been too kind to Frost, principally because there is little sign of development in his work, and also because he rarely experimented with form and line, giving a conventional feel to much of his output. However, this assessment underestimates his ear for common speech, and at his best there is a spare, meditative quality to his lyrics.

Selected Poems
Penguin pbk £6.99

collection of 1961, *Kaddish,* was a move towards incorporating material from his family history, particularly his mother's insanity, into his poetry and the results, in the title poem and others, were moving and powerful. Ginsberg has continued to write and perform poetry, to sing the joys of mind-altering drugs, of gay sex and of Blakean mysticism with an energy and enthusiasm that are endearing but it is clear that his best work was in the fifties and sixties, that he was a poet of particular historical moments and that, outside these moments, he runs a constant danger of self-parody.

Collected Poems
Penguin pbk £17.00

Howl and other Poems
City Lights pbk £10.99

Graham, Jorie
(1951 -)

Jorie Graham was born in New York and grew up in Italy; she was educated at the Sorbonne and in America. She teaches currently at the Iowa Writers' Workshop, the best known creative writing programme in the United States. Graham's earliest collection displayed a precocious talent and were most successful exploring the poet's rapturous celebration of the natural world . With her third volume, *The End of Beauty* (1987) her poetry became more radically interiorised and structurally disjunctive. Her idiosyncratic adoption of free verse forms via Whitman, Pound and Charles Olson tended towards the ecstatic or trance-like, the details and texture of the objective world retreating within a dazzling cascade of reactions to the world. It is the movement of the poet's mind that becomes the subject of the poem and at her best Graham reveals the poetry of the moment exactly and beautifully. Her work is preoccupied with language, meaning and identity; it is a poetry of liberation from the everyday which at times is unashamedly difficult to read. Championed by Helen Vendler, the high priestess of poetry criticism in America, as an addition to the growing canon of American poetry and hailed by John Ashbery as one of the 'finest poets writing today', Jorie Graham was awarded the Pulitzer Prize for her *Selected Poems: The Dream of a Unified Field* (1996).

The Dream of the Unified Field
Carcanet pbk £12.95

Hughes, Langston
(1902 - 1967)

Hughes was amongst the leading figures of the Harlem Renaissance, the flowering of black creativity in Twenties New York and his output of drama, fiction, autobiography and libretti was enormous. His success in bringing the African-American experience and the rhythms of black speech and music into the mainstream literary tradition was highly influential.

Selected Poems
Serpent's Tail pbk £8.99

Jeffers, Robinson
(1887 - 1962)

From the perspective of the late twentieth century Jeffers remains as one of the least integrated figures in American poetry. Undoubtedly a major figure, the harshness, austerity and classicism of his poetry stand in contrast to many of his contemporaries. Two of the main influences on him were his diverse but essentially classical education and his settling in the remote Monterey mountains on the California coast, from which he drew much inspiration for the symbolism of rock and stone which is everywhere in his work.

Selected Poems
Carcanet pbk £6.95

Kees, Weldon
(1914 - 1955)

Kees conducted a versatile career as essayist, journalist, novelist, jazz pianist, painter, film-maker and, chiefly, poet. He is noted for a relatively small body of work, available in this country in *Collected Poems* which, as Donald Justice remarks, are best appreciated through the 'cumulative power of the work as a whole'. He is perhaps best known for the 'Robinson' poems, touching on the life of his 'typical man' with 'his sad and usual heart'. Kees' voice is by turns satirical, apocalyptic, deadpan and seductive, with the power to draw the reader deep into the strange, bleak world of his imaginative territory. In 1955 Kees vanished, leaving his car parked near the Golden Gate Bridge.

Collected Poems
Faber pbk £7.99

Kerouac, Jack
(1922 - 1969)

Kerouac - novelist, drinker, dharma bum - is a legendary figure and *On the Road* remains a talismanic text to many people, discovered by new generations to whom it speaks as directly as it did to the Beat generation of the fifties. His poetry is slight but, in its own way, affecting. Swiftly thought, instantly written, immediately accessible, his poems are largely uninterested in form - although he does demonstrate an interest in haiku - but Kerouac's romantic vision of total and honest communication between individuals, between writer and reader has its appeal.

Pomes All Sizes
City Lights pbk £7.99

Scattered Poems
City Lights pbk £4.50

Levertov, Denise
(1923 -)

Unique amongst American poets in being born and raised in Ilford, Essex, Levertov moved to the States after the war and became an American citizen in 1955. Her poetry, although sometimes recalling her Essex upbringing, owes little to the English tradition, being influenced much more by the Objectivists and the Black Mountain poets. She has built her considerable reputation through regularly published collections over the last forty years, producing poetry that has placed her personal and political concerns within a larger spiritual context.

Selected Poems
Bloodaxe pbk £8.95

Longfellow, Henry Wadsworth (1807 - 1882)

In his lifetime Longfellow was one of the most widely read poets in the English-speaking world and poems such as *The Wreck of the Hesperus* and *The Village Blacksmith* are familiar to succeeding generations through classroom recitation and regular anthologisation. His most famous work, *The Song of Hiawatha,* an attempt to create a peculiarly American mythology through the story of an Indian warrior and statesman, remains popular although the incantatory metre in which the narrative was told has attracted many parodies.

Selected Poems
Dent pbk £2.95

Lowell, Robert
(1917 - 1977)

A member of a distinguished Boston family, grandson of the 19th century writer of the same name, Lowell converted to Catholicism after his first marriage and his early work is marked by Catholic symbolism and by his quest for spiritual values within his new faith. Yet it also shows a high level of inventiveness in syntax and rhythm. His most famous collection, *Life Studies,* draws heavily on autobiographical material and is one of the central works of the 'confessional' style of writing. Lowell is open about his darkest personal experiences, his periods in mental hospitals and the difficulties of his marriages. Later collections continued to include poetry in the confessional mode but he was also drawn by his very vocal opposition to the Vietnam War to produce poetry that examined public as well as private events.

Selected Poems
Faber pbk £5.99

Lynch, Thomas

Thomas Lynch combines his work as a poet with work as an undertaker in Michigan and his daily proximity to death informs the wise, compassionate and large-hearted poetry in his collection *Grimalkin & Other Poems*. Writing of the basic experiences of love and death, grief and desire in a language that is direct and immediate, Lynch disguises the skill and technical facility he employs to produce a voice that speaks to the reader with power, precision and a wry, mordant humour.

Grimalkin & Other Poems
Cape pbk £7.00

The Old Operating Theatre, London, All Souls Night
by Thomas Lynch

To rooms like this old resurrectionists
returned the bodies they had disinterred -
fresh corpses so fledgling anatomists
could study Origin and Insertion points
of deltoids, pecs, trapezius and count
the vertebrae, the ball & socket joints.
And learn the private parts and Latin names
by which the heart becomes a myocardium,
the high cheek bone a zygoma, the brain,
less prone to daydream as a cerebellum.

And squirming in their stiff, unflinching seats,
apprentice surgeons witnessed in the round,
new methods in advanced colostomy,
the amputation of gangrenous limbs
and watched as Viennese lobotomists
banished the ravings of a raving man
but left him scarred and drooling in a way
that made them wonder was he much improved?
But here the bloodied masters taught dispassionate
incisions - how to suture and remove.

In rooms like this, the Greeks and Romans staged
their early dramas. Early Christians knelt
and hummed their liturgies when it was held
that prayer and penance were the only potions.
Ever since Abraham, guided by God,
first told his tribesmen of the deal he'd made -
their foreskins for that ancient Covenant -
good medicine's meant letting human blood.
Good props include the table and the blade.
Good theatre is knowing where to cut.

Merrill, James
(1926 -)

Regarded in America as a major poet, to be ranked with Lowell and Ashbery, Merrill has not gained the reputation he deserves in Britain. The scion of a wealthy family, Merrill was able to travel widely and wrote much about his journeys abroad, particularly his experiences in the Mediterranean culture of Greece. His major work was a massive sequence *The Changing of Light at Sandover*, written in an astonishing array of styles, in which the poet communicates via ouija board with departed friends, including Auden, who lead him and his companion towards spiritual understanding. The same technical control and inventiveness, which mark the longer poems, are to be found in the shorter poems of his other collections.

Selected Poems,
Carcanet pbk £12.95

Moore, Marianne
(1887 - 1972)

Marianne Moore was born in St. Louis, Missouri but lived in New York from 1918, where she worked, for some years, on the prestigious literary periodical *The Dial*. Her early work, much praised by Ezra Pound amongst others, was collected in her first volume, published in 1921 and further collections followed as she gained greater recognition and built her reputation to the point where she was acknowledged as the leading American woman poet of her generation. Her *Collected Poems*, published in 1952, won the Pulitzer Prize, the National Book Award and the Bollingen Award in the one year. Hers is a poetry that values virtues like grace and self-sufficiency - reflected in the fact that many of her best poems are about animals, athletes and practitioners of daring and dangerous trades - and is written in lines that observe a strict syllabic count rather than any conventional metre. Her famous dictum about poetry - that poets should present 'imaginary gardens with real toads in them' - demonstrates her devotion to facts, a devotion such that she often incorporates in her work, unaltered, quotations from encyclopedias, dictionaries and magazines and once included an index in one of her collections.

Complete Poems
Faber pbk £9.99

O'Hara, Frank
(1926 - 1966)

O'Hara was employed by the Museum of Modern Art in New York and was deeply involved in the art world of the city, espousing the work of Abstract Expressionists such as Jackson Pollock and Willem de Kooning. His poetry celebrates the energies of urban life and the accidents and contingencies which pervade it.

Selected Poems
Carcanet hbk £18.95

Olson, Charles
(1910 -1970)

As rector of Black Mountain College in North Carolina, Olson was the guiding light of the Black Mountain poets who include Robert Creeley, Denise Levertov and Robert Duncan. They were all influenced by Olson's demand for what he called 'Projectivist Verse', a poetry in which the poem is seen as an 'open field' through which the energy of the language moves and the verse form is determined by the breath of the speaker-poet, rather than by metrical feet. His major work is the *The Maximus Poems* in which the past and present of Olson's hometown are refracted through the persona of Maximus, a disenchanted observer of contemporary culture.

The Maximus Poems
University of California Press pbk £28.00

Plath, Sylvia
(1932 - 1963)

Sylvia Plath has been described by Al Alvarez as 'one of the most powerful and lavishly gifted poets of our time.' In her lifetime she published only one collection *The Colossus* and her novel *The Bell Jar* and her work only gained attention after her death in 1963. Plath's posthumous fame rests largely on the later poems collected in *Ariel*, written during an intensely creative period immediately prior to her death. Often inhabiting a surreal psychic landscape, Plath's poems are characterised by her charged imagery of father, bees, cadaver, sea, birth, moon and death and ultimately by the originality and skill of a writer whose posthumous literary impact has been enormous.

Ariel
Faber pbk £5.99

Collected Poems
Faber pbk £11.99

Selected Poems
Faber pbk £6.99

Pound, Ezra
(1885 - 1972)

Ezra Pound is the most controversial writer of the twentieth century and few other writers have excited such contradictory judgments. He was, as T.S. Eliot said, 'more responsible for the 20th Century revolution in poetry than any other individual', both as poet himself and as encourager and discoverer of other talents. After he moved away from the spare clarity of Imagism, he found a new freedom through translation - from Provencal troubadours, from Old English and from classical Chinese. His masterpiece is *The Cantos*, a massive work on which he worked intermittently for fifty years. They are difficult poems because of their huge range of reference and their assimilation of material from many cultures, their combination of different linguistic registers, languages and parallel historical worlds but they must be counted among the great achievements of twentieth century poetry. His last decades were overshadowed by the tragedy consequent upon his arrest for broadcasts he made for Italian radio during the war and the twelve years of incarceration in a mental institution.

Cantos of Ezra Pound
Faber pbk £20.00

Selected Cantos
Faber pbk £8.99

Selected Poems
Faber pbk £7.99

Poe, Edgar Allan
(1809 - 1849)

Orphaned at an early age, Poe was raised by a guardian and lived as a child in England for five years. His chequered career after leaving the University of Virginia included a period in the US Army and a prolonged struggle to earn a living as a freelance writer and journalist. He died in Baltimore several days after being found, delirious from alcohol and illness, on the street. Poe is best remembered for such tales of mystery and imagination as *The Fall of the House of Usher* and *Murders in the Rue Morgue* but he wrote and published a great deal of verse, much of it demonstrating the same macabre fascination with the occult and the pathological evinced in his short stories. His most famous poem remains *The Raven*. His admirers have included Baudelaire, who translated his work into French, Oscar Wilde, Yeats and Freud.

Complete Tales and Poems
Penguin pbk £11.00

Selected Poems and Essays
Everyman pbk £5.99

Rexroth, Kenneth
(1905 - 1982)

Rexroth was born in Indiana but lived most of his adult life in San Francisco where he involved himself in most of the American literary movements from the Thirties onwards, from the Objectivists to the Beats and beyond. He was also an active sympathiser with the American left and some of his verse, although not his best, reflects his angry hatred of all forms of oppression. Perhaps his best work is to be found in his translations from Chinese and Japanese poetry where his absorption in the task of rendering the sense of stillness in the originals quietens the stridency to which his own verse was liable.

100 Poems fom the Chinese
New Directions pbk £6.35

Rich, Adrienne
(1929 -)

Adrienne Rich's father taught his daughter complex poetic metres and rhyme schemes at an early age, and she published a collection of verse in her early twenties, but she sought to move away from traditional poetic devices towards freer forms derived from Whitman, Pound and William Carlos Williams. When she married, Rich found the constraints placed upon wives and mothers in Eisenhower's America difficult and her work often displays an anger and resentment towards her confinement as a writer during these years. It was only in the sixties that she began to break free from the restraints and her work as a poet parallels her growth and independence within the development of a wider feminist consciousness. Her poetry since has often been directly autobiographical, drawing upon her experience of being Jewish and lesbian in a changing America, and has frequently undermined the iconography of domestic heterosexuality.

Collected Early Poems
Norton pbk £10.95

Dark Fields of the Republic
Norton pbk £7.50

Diving into the Wreck
Norton pbk £6.95

Roethke, Theodore
(1908 - 1963)

A native of Michigan, Roethke drew the backcloth and symbolic material for much of his poetry from the North Western landscape. At his best, his ability to synthesise nature and the unconscious mind created uniquely quirky and arresting lyrics which set him apart from any movement. This was formally recognised in 1953, when *The Waking* was awarded a Pulitzer Prize, although it is widely felt that the posthumous volume, *The Far Field* (1964) contains his most successful poems, poems in which he experimented with longer line length, and freer metres.

Collected Poems
Faber pbk £11.99

Sexton, Anne
(1928 - 1974)

The publication of Anne Sexton's first collection in 1960 marked her as an early exponent of what critics, referring particularly to Robert Lowell, were to call 'confessional' poetry. She went on to publish a number of other collections including *Live or Die*, which won the Pulitzer Prize in 1967, before committing suicide by carbon monoxide poisoning in 1974. Sexton began writing poetry as part of her psychiatric treatment for a breakdown she suffered after the birth of her second daughter and her work explores her disturbed life through images of pain, adultery, loneliness and madness. In the best of her poems she brings great force and imaginative energy to bear on her examinations of the darker side of the psyche.

Selected Poems
Virago pbk £8.99

Stevens, Wallace
(1879 - 1955)

Wallace Stevens was born in Reading, Pennsylvania, educated at Harvard and spent most of his life in Hartford, Connecticut, working as a successful executive in an insurance company. His other life was poetry and it is probably fair to say that he developed the most rigorous aesthetic of any American poet. His theme is broadly that art elaborates analogues for experience which, properly understood, give life its deepest meaning. The poems themselves deploy a classically resonant language to explore philosophical themes in an ideal landscape, and often have the kind of subtle, modulated beauty suggested by the title he gave to one of his later collections, *The Auroras of Autumn*.

Collected Poems
Faber pbk £14.99

Selected Poems
Faber pbk £7.99

Stevenson, Anne
(1933 -)

Although Anne Stevenson was born in England, and lives here now, she was brought up in the USA. Her *Selected Poems* demonstrates the range of her work - she has written both psychologically acute observations of human behaviour and lyrically evocative pieces on the natural world and landscapes as different as the Fenlands and the Sierra Nevada - and she has since published further collections. One of her most interesting works is the ambitious sequence *Correspondences* which traces the history of a New England family over a century and a half. Stevenson ingeniously uses the form of personal letters from members of the family to reveal the ways in which the moral puritanism of the original family patriarch continues to affect his descendants. She has also written a controversial biography of Sylvia Plath.

Collected Poems
Oxford UP pbk £15.00

Walker, Alice
(1944 -)

Although Alice Walker is best known for her novels, particularly the Pulitzer prizewinning *The Color Purple*, her first publications were collections of poems based on her experiences in the civil rights movement of the sixties and her travels in Africa. She has since published further volumes of accessible poetry celebrating the basic emotions of love, motherhood and friendship and honouring those who have struggled against racism.

Her Blue Body Everything We Know : Complete Poems
Women's Press pbk £9.99

Whitman, Walt
(1819 - 1892)

Whitman's early adulthood was a combination of printing, teaching and eventually journalism in New York and Brooklyn. He had inherited radical democratic ideas and the increasingly confident articulation of his political views brought him into conflict with a number of editors. Around the time of the publication of the first edition of *Leaves of Grass* (1855), he struck out on his own, recreating himself consciously as a bardic figure for an increasingly self-confident New World, a role which in time became the man. His experiences in the Civil War, when he worked as a nurse in army hospitals, affected him deeply and were reflected in the poems published as *Drum-Taps* and later incorporated into editions of *Leaves of Grass*. In all, *Leaves of Grass* went through nine editions, being added to with each edition, and is now generally considered to be an enduring masterpiece. It is sprawling, ambitious in its themes, inclusive and brave, both in the way it breaks all established rules of metre and rhythm, and also in its embracing of sexual themes, for which Whitman was predictably pilloried by his contemporaries. His work, and the persona he created, have proven enormously liberating for many of his American successors from Hart Crane to the Beat generation and beyond.

Complete Poems
Penguin pbk

Leaves of Grass
Penguin pbk £4.99

Leaves of Grass
Norton pbk £10.95

Wilbur, Richard
(1921 -)

Wilbur began writing poetry while serving with the American army in the Second World War and his first collection was published in 1947. His poetry stands separate from the modern confessional, individualistic tradition exemplified by Robert Lowell. His favourite subjects and themes derive from his apprehension of the splendours of the physical world and an underlying, unseen spiritual order. The formal metres and painstakingly rhymed stanzas are frequently described as 'urbane' and 'elegant'. The reader requires no special glossary or biographical crib to understand his work. 'Poems', he has stated, ' are conflicts with disorder not messages from one person to another.' (This certitude has led some critics to claim that his work has not 'developed'.) *Things of This World* (1956)

won both the Pulitzer Prize and a National Book Award and in 1987 he was named as the second poet laureate of the United States. His New and Collected Poems was published in 1988.

New and Collected Poems
Faber pbk £9.99

Williams, C.K.
(1936 -)

C. K. Williams is the most challenging American poet of his generation and his poetry, published in several collections since its first appearance in the sixties, is intensely original in its capacity to engage with the realities of urban life, the psychological dramas of marriage, family and friendship and the blighted lives of those whom the American dream has eluded. As one critic has noted, 'one has the feeling, unusual when reading today's poets, that he is truly interested in the lives around him' and his urgent narratives and uncompromising portraits are embodied in a verse that employs to great effect a rich and complex syntax and the long unrhymed line that is his hallmark.

New and Selected Poems
Bloodaxe pbk £9.95

Williams, W. Carlos
(1833 - 1963)

Initially trained as a doctor, Williams followed both a medical and literary career. As a student, he met Pound and H.D. and was a sympathiser (although not strictly a member) of the Imagist movement, dominated by the poetics articulated by T.E. Hulme. Williams shared with them a yearning for a poetry that was rooted in objective truth and which he probably crystallised better than any of his contemporaries in his famous edict "no ideas but in things." Alongside this was another preoccupation of his, which was for the colour and character of common life, and the combination of his poetic and thematic guiding principles results in a body of work, which, especially in its earlier phase, reads with disarming simplicity to the modern reader. However, his rejection of conventional metrical patterns in favour of following his own voice patterns marked him out as an especially experimental writer in his own time. The high point of Williams' poetic career came with the long poem *Paterson*, which was published in five books between 1946 and 1958. Paterson is simultaneously a city and a man, and the synthesis achieved in the poem between the personal and the public is superbly realised.

Collected Poems 1909-1939
Carcanet pbk £6.95

Collected Poems 1939-1962
Carcanet pbk £6.95

Selected Poems 1939-1962
Penguin pbk £7.99

Time: 1975
by C.K. Williams

My father-in-law is away, Catherine and I and Renee, her mother,
        are eating in the kitchen;
Jed, three weeks old, sleeps in his floppy straw cradle on the
        counter next to the bread box;
we've just arrived, and I'm so weary with jet lag, with the labor
        of tending to a newborn
that my mind drifts and, instead of their words, I listen to the
        music of the women's voices.

Some family business must be being resolved : Renee is agitated,
        her tone suddenly urgent,
there's something she's been waiting to tell; her eyes hold on
        Catherine's and it's that,
the intensity of her gaze, that brings back to me how Catherine
        looked during her labor -
all those hours - then, the image startlingly vivid, I see Renee
        giving birth to Catherine.

I see the darkened room, then the bed, then, sinews drawn tight
        in her neck, Renee herself,
with the same abstracted look in her eyes that Catherine had,
        layer on layer of self disadhering,
all the dross gone, all but the fire of concentration, the heart-
        stopping beauty, and now,
at last, my Catherine, our Catherine, here for us all, blazing,
        lacquered with gore.

Classical Verse

Hesiod
(c. 800 B.C.)

Hesiod was the earliest of the Greek poets after Homer. His major work *Works and Days* is an account of the operations of the farming year and of the astrologically favourable and unfavourable days within it, interspersed with much country lore and with stories taken from the common store of Greek mythology.

Works and Days
Penguin pbk £6.99

This herm is a Roman copy of an ideal portrait of the Hellenistic period, showing the poet Homer as a blind old man

© The British Museum

Homer
(c. 800 B.C.)

The works of Homer - the *Iliad,* the story of the war between the Greeks and the Trojans, and the *Odyssey,* the account of Odysseus and his epic journey back from the war to his homeland - mark the beginning of literature in the West and have been continuously influential for more than two and a half millennia. There has been much debate about the date of Homer, about whether or not the two works are the works of one individual, of two individuals or the gathering together of verses by countless anonymous bards. There was even a debate in the last century, begun by Samuel Butler, about whether Homer was a man or a woman. What has never been a matter of debate is the beauty of the

Sappho
(BORN C. 612 B.C.)

Sappho, born of aristocratic parentage on the island of Lesbos, was the dominating figure in a circle of women held together by shared emotional sensibilities and a devotion to poetry. Only a handful of her poems survive but she was one of the originators of the subjective personal lyric, a tradition handed on to the Roman poets Catullus and Horace, amongst others, developed by countless poets through the centuries and still very much alive today.

Poems and Fragments
Bloodaxe pbk £7.95

Theocritus
(C. 310 - 250 B.C.)

Theocritus, born in Sicily, was the source of the genre of pastoral poetry which has had such a long and diverse history in European literature. Later developments in the genre led to the artificiality of rural lives being celebrated by sophisticated urban poets but the real peasant culture of Sicily and South Italy at the time lies behind Theocritus' verse.

Idylls
Penguin pbk £6.95

verse in both poems and the centrality of both to European literature. The most famous verse translations are those of Chapman, an inspiration to Keats, and Pope. Contemporary versions in verse include Christopher Logue's translations of selected passages and Richmond Lattimore's rendering of the Iliad. The standard prose version is E. V. Rieu's translation for Penguin Classics.

The Iliad
(trans. Rieu)
Penguin pbk £5.95

The Iliad
(trans. Fitzgerald)
Oxford UP pbk £4.95

The Odyssey
(trans. Rieu)
Penguin pbk £4.95

The Odyssey (trans. Shewring)
Oxford UP pbk £5.95

The Odyssey
(trans. Fitzgerald)
Harvill pbk £7.95

(Logue) War Music
Faber pbk £6.99

(Logue) Kings
Faber pbk £5.99

Homer in English (ed. Steiner)
Penguin pbk £9.99

Catullus
(C. 84 - 54 B. C.)

The immediacy and spontaneity of Catullus' poetry, particularly the sequence of love lyrics addressed to his mistress 'Lesbia', and the range of emotion evoked, from emotional fulfilment to bitter rejection, made his work enormously influential on the development of the Latin lyric and also on European literature since the Middle Ages.

Poems
Penguin pbk £6.99

Horace
(65 - 8 B. C.)

Like his friend Virgil, Horace was a member of the literary circle surrounding Augustus' minister Maecenas. His works range from odes in imitation of the Greek lyricists through an influential statement of aesthetic principles in *Ars Poetica* to a sequence of gentle and ironic satires from which emerges a portrait of the author, his likes and dislikes, his quirks and prejudices. Horace has always been one of the most widely read of the Latin poets.

Odes and Epodes
Penguin pbk £7.50

Satires
Penguin pbk £6.99

Horace in English
(ed. Carne-Ross)
Penguin pbk £9.99

Lucretius
(c.99 - 55 B.C.)

Lucretius' chief work is *De Rerum Natura,* a philosophical poem in which he aims to show how the ideas of the Greek philosopher Epicurus can free men from the tyranny of the fear of death. The poem follows an intellectually complex argument but also uses a wealth of illustrative material and rich metaphor to embody its ideas.

On the Nature of the Universe
Penguin pbk £6.99

Juvenal
(c.60 - 136 A.D.)

Juvenal is the greatest of the Roman satirists and his exercises in rhetorical condemnation of the vices of his age are in marked contrast to the urbanity of Horace's satires. The vigour with which Juvenal portrayed the degeneracies he anathematised is striking and his work has affected all satirists since.

Sixteen Satires
Penguin pbk £7.99

Martial
(c.40 - 104)

Born in Spain, Martial lived largely in Rome during the years in which he was writing the 1,500 short poems on which his reputation rests. His epigrammatic verse is largely satirical, often bawdy, and indeed our own concept of the epigram as a compact witticism with a sting in its tail derives ultimately from Martial.

Epigrams
Penguin pbk £6.99

Martial in English
(ed. Sullivan & Boyle)
Penguin pbk £9.99

Ovid

(43 B.C. - A.D. 18)

Ovid wrote in a wide range of verse forms and was a leading figure in the literary world of his time before, for slightly mysterious reasons, the emperor Augustus banished him to the remote Black Sea port of Tomis. His love elegies, *Amores*, have been long influential but his greatest work is the *Metamorphoses*, a sequence of tales from mythology loosely linked by the theme of shape-changing.

Erotic Poems
Penguin pbk £8.99

Heroides
Penguin pbk £6.99

Metamorphoses
Penguin pbk £7.99

Poems of Exile
Penguin pbk £7.99

Persius

(A.D. 34 - 62)

The satires of Persius were directed at the excesses of the court under Nero and much influenced by Stoic thinking. In the past they have been translated by Dryden and the edition now in print is translated by the American poet W. S. Merwin.

Satires of Persius
(trans. Merwin)
Anvil Press pbk £6.95

Virgil

(70 - 19 B.C.)

The greatest of all Latin poets, Virgil produced work in a number of genres borrowed from Greek literature but successfully reworked them into distinctively Roman creations. *The Eclogues*, written within the tradition that began with Theocritus, are poems of escape into an idealised pastoral world, although some of them carry hints and implications of a real world beyond the arcadian pursuits of shepherds and goatherds. *The Georgics* are very loosely indebted to Hesiod but move beyond didacticism into a rich celebration of life in the Italian countryside. His great epic, *The Aeneid,* which tells the story of Aeneas' escape from Troy, his adventures en route to Italy and his foundation of the Roman state, uses the form as a means of presenting a great patriotic myth and of linking the legendary figures of the past with the Roman history that had culminated in Virgil's imperial patron Augustus.

The Aeneid
(trans. Fitzgerald)
Harvill £5.95

The Aeneid
(trans. Knight)
Penguin pbk £3.99

The Aeneid
(trans. C. Day-Lewis)
Oxford UP pbk £4.95

The Eclogues
Penguin pbk £4.95

The Georgics
Penguin pbk £4.95

Virgil in English
(ed. Gransden)
Penguin pbk £8.99

Poetry in Translation

Akhmatova, Anna
(1889 - 1966)

Akhmatova was an early member of the Acmeists, a group of Russian poets in the period immediately before the First World War which also included her husband Gumilev, later executed on charges of participation in an anti-Soviet conspiracy, and Osip Mandelstam. Her early collections aimed at bringing the clarity and precision the Acmeists admired to the description of love and personal feelings. Under the Soviet regime she was not allowed to publish for many years - her poetry was considered too personal and insufficiently political - but she continued to write, beginning her cycle of poems occasioned by the Stalinist terror and the threat it offered to her own family. From 1940 to 1962 she worked on her greatest achievement, *Poem Without a Hero,* a tremendous meditation on time and suffering woven around the central tragedy of a poet's suicide.

Selected Poems
Bloodaxe pbk £6.95

Selected Poems
Penguin pbk £6.99

Apollinaire, Guillaume
(1880 - 1918)

A prominent figure in avant-garde circles in Paris, Apollinaire was a friend of the cubists, including Picasso, and a frequent contributor to the ephemeral little magazines of the period before the war. He fought and was wounded in the war and died in the influenza epidemic of 1918. His poetry is marked by its experimental energy and by his typographic ingenuity and inventiveness - one poem in the collection *Calligrammes,* called *Il pleut,* is printed with the letters trickling like water down the page.

Selected Poems
Anvil Press pbk £8.95

Calligram *Mirror.*

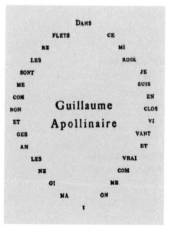

Ariosto, Ludovico
(1474 - 1535)

Ariosto, although he also wrote plays and satires, is now remembered primarily for his epic poem *Orlando Furioso* which he began to write in the first decade of the sixteenth century and continued to revise for the rest of his life. The first edition was published in Venice in 1516. Designed to honour the house of Este, in whose service Ariosto spent much of his life, and its exalted ancestry, *Orlando Furioso* tells the story of a knight in Charlemagne's service, his unrequited love which drives him into madness and the war between Christians and Saracens for possession of Europe.

Orlando Furioso
Oxford UP pbk £8.99

Baudelaire, Charles
(1821 - 1867)

Baudelaire's poetic genius was little appreciated during his lifetime but the one collection he published, *Les Fleurs du Mal*, can now be seen as probably the most important collection of French verse in the nineteenth century. On its first publication in 1857 Baudelaire and his publisher were prosecuted for offences against public decency and six poems ordered to be excised from future editions, a ban that was not officially lifted until 1949. Baudelaire's determination to extract poetic beauty from a world largely seen as ugly and evil, his lingering over that ugliness and evil and his search for inspiration in the secret life of the streets of Paris have been enormously influential in the years since his death. Although Baudelaire used classically correct metrical forms, he introduced a new, distinctively modern sensibility into French verse.

Complete Poems Volume 1
Anvil Press pbk £8.95

Complete Poems Volume 2
Anvil Press pbk £8.95

Les Fleurs du Mal
Oxford UP pbk £6.95

Selected Poems
Penguin pbk £6.99

Brodsky, Joseph
(1940 - 1996)

His early poetry won Brodsky a reputation on the Leningrad literary scene but he fell foul of the regime and spent periods of time in Soviet jails for alleged social parasitism. Eventually, in 1972, he went into exile from the Soviet Union and lived the rest of his life in the USA, working at a number of universities there. His lyric and elegiac poetry, with its concerns for the fundamental questions of life, death and the search for meaning in existence, won him the Nobel Prize for Literature in 1987. Brodsky's exile from his own country and from his language are reflected in the poetry, although he became a fluent translator of work into English and he cooperated with a number of distinguished American poets including Anthony Hecht and Richard Wilbur on translations.

Part of Speech
Oxford UP pbk £5.99

Camoes, Luis de
(1524 -1580)

Camoes is the great national poet of Portugal and his epic *The Lusiads,* which tells the story of Vasco da Gama's discovery of the sea route to India, is a work which helped the expanding Portuguese nation to define itself. Little is known for certain about the poet but he may well have been an impoverished member of the old aristocracy who spent his life in service to the newly developed Portuguese empire.

The Lusiads
Penguin pbk £6.99

Cavafy, Constantine
(1863 - 1933)

Cavafy came to the attention of the English-reading world through the advocacy of E.M. Forster who met him in Cavafy's native Alexandria and maintained a long friendship and correspondence with him. His poetry is divided between personal lyrics which celebrate his homosexual affairs with, for the time, great frankness and verse on subjects taken from the rich past of the classical and hellenistic period, viewed through ironic and sceptical eyes.

Collected Poems
Chatto pbk £9.99

Celan, Paul
(1920 - 1970)

Celan was the pseudonym of Paul Anschel, born in present-day Romania of a Jewish family. He lost both his parents in the Holocaust and was himself imprisoned in a labour camp for two years. After the war he settled in Paris where he taught and where he finally drowned himself in the Seine. He wrote his poetry in German. George Steiner has referred to Celan as 'almost certainly the major European poet of the period after 1945' and his difficult and demanding verse is an uncompromising attempt to encompass what can and cannot be said in poetry about the horrors of the century.

Selected Poems
Penguin pbk £8.99

Dante
(1265 - 1321)

Born into a family of the Florentine nobility, Dante was active in the complicated factional politics of his native city and was eventually exiled from the city when a rival faction to his own came to power. He spent the rest of his life wandering from Italian city state to Italian city state, eventually dying at Ravenna. *La Vita Nuova,* dating from the early 1290s, is a collection of poems, most of them relating his idealised love for Beatrice, a woman not certainly identified but probably Beatrice Portinari whose death in 1290 threw Dante into spiritual turmoil. His greatest work, and one of the greatest works of European literature, is the *Divine Comedy,* the story of the poet's journey through the various stages of the afterlife, guided by the poet Virgil through Hell and Purgatory and introduced by Beatrice to the transcendent spiritual heights of Paradise.

Divine Comedy
Oxford UP pbk £8.99

Divine Comedy Vol 1: Inferno
Penguin pbk £6.99

Divine Comedy Vol 2: Purgatory
Penguin pbk £6.99

Divine Comedy Vol 3: Paradise
Penguin pbk £6.99

Eluard, Paul
(1895 - 1952)

Eluard was linked with the surrealist movement in 1920s Paris and wrote volumes in collaboration with André Breton, the 'pope of Surrealism' and with the painter Max Ernst. He broke with surrealism in the thirties and joined the Communist party during the war, becoming one of the leading figures in the intellectual resistance to German occupation.

Unbroken Poetry II
Bloodaxe pbk £8.95

Dante

Enzensberger, Hans Magnus
(1929 -)

Perhaps Germany's greatest living poet, Enzensberger was born in Bavaria and grew up in Nuremberg during the Third Reich. His often satirical poetry is imbued with his political and moral concerns, his desire to draw upon the radical critiques of Marxism without sacrificing the freedoms it has so often ignored. *Kiosk,* his latest collection, sees him disillusioned with public issues, yet insistent still upon their inescapable importance, and prepared to draw more fully on his personal experiences. He has also written many cultural and political essays, some of which have been translated into English.

Kiosk
Bloodaxe pbk £7.95

Selected Poems
Bloodaxe pbk £8.95

Eschenbach, Wolfram von
(C. 1170 - C. 1220)

An impoverished Bavarian knight who wrote two of the great epics of Middle High German poetry. *Willehalm* is the unfinished story of the crusader William of Orange and *Parzival,* an account of the Arthurian knight's passage from ignorance and naivete to a state of spiritual grace

Parzival
Penguin pbk £8.99

Willehalm
Penguin pbk £7.99

Esenin, Sergei
(1895 - 1925)

Esenin was born into a peasant family in Russia and his tempestuous life, fuelled by drink and excess, ended in suicide. He wrote his last poem in his own blood. Originally an enthusiast for the October Revolution, he grew rapidly disillusioned and the brutal lyrics of his aptly titled collection, *Confessions of a Hooligan,* are the result.

Confessions of a Hooligan
Carcanet hbk £8.95

France, Marie de
(c.1160-c.1190)

The earliest known French woman poet, Marie de France, in all likelihood, wrote her twelve *Lais,* a series of narratives told in Anglo-Norman couplets, while living in England. Almost nothing is known certainly of her life.

Lais of Marie de France
Penguin pbk £5.99

Goethe, J. Wolfgang v.
(1749-1832)

The publication of his novel *The Sorrows of Young Werther* in 1774, with its archetypal romantic hero, sensitive and ill-fated, brought Goethe great fame throughout Europe and he remained astonishingly creative and productive for the rest of his life. During his long career in the service of the Duke of Weimar he published plays, most famously the poetic drama in two parts *Faust,* novels and short stories, travel writings, essays and scientific research.
Throughout his life he wrote and published lyric poetry drawn from his own emotional life - 'fragments of a great confession', as he referred to all his creative work - and ballads such as the well known *Erl -King* drawn from rich Germanic traditions.

Roman Elegies
Libris P pbk £12.95

Selected Poems
John Calder pbk £9.95

Selected Poems
Penguin pbk £7.99

Heine, Heinrich
(1797 - 1856)

Heine was born of a Jewish family but converted to Protestantism in an unsuccessful attempt to gain entry into professions barred to Jews at the time. His liberal views led him, in 1831, to move to Paris after he had despaired of significant radical change in the German states and he lived there for the rest of his life, originally in voluntary exile but later unable to return permanently to his native land because his political and satirical writings had fallen foul of the censors. He is now best remembered as a lyric poet - one whose works have been set to music by very nearly every German composer of note - and his first collection *Buch der Lieder (Book of Songs),* with its combination of romantic melancholy and an ironic awareness of the posturing inherent in such romanticism, has been one of the most widely read and influential books in German literature.

Selected Verse
Penguin pbk £6.99

Herbert, Zbigniew
(1924 -)

Herbert was born in Lvov, then part of Poland and began writing poetry in his teens, although he published little until the mid-fifties. Widely read and deeply embedded in the European cultural tradition, Herbert has been described by Czeslaw Milosz as a 'poet of historical irony'. He achieves some kind of uncertain equilibrium in his verse by investing the cycles of history with discernible patterns despite the horrors, although he himself has said that he approaches history 'not for lessons in hope but to confront my experiences with the experiences of others.'

Mr Cogito
Oxford Up pbk £7.99

Hölderlin, Friedrich
(1770 - 1843)

Hölderlin's greatest achievement was to adapt classical verse forms to his native German, employing them to express his romantic longings for what he saw as an ancient Greek harmony with the natural world, a harmony lost to him and his contemporaries. His great tragedy was the mental illness that overwhelmed him in the first decade of the nineteenth century and overshadowed completely the last thirty five years of his life.

Selected Poems
Bloodaxe pbk £8.99

Selected Verse
Anvil Press pbk £7.95

Holub, Miroslav
(1923 -)

Born in Pilsen, Czechoslovakia, Holub has been described by Ted Hughes as 'one of the half dozen most important poets writing anywhere'. Undoubtedly the Czech Republic's foremost poet, he is also a leading scientist. In *Poems Before and After : Collected English Translations,* the poems written in the claustrophobic pre-1968 climate are often expressed allegorically in lean, free forms suffused with Holub's mordant wit, while the poems of After show a movement to more expansive and dramatic structures. Holub's wide-ranging intelligence combines the scientific, philosophical, historical and mythological to form a poetry of great significance and originality.

Poems Before and After
Bloodaxe pbk £9.95

Laforgue, Jules
(1860 - 1887)

The characteristics of
Laforgue, who died young
from tuberculosis, are irony,
self-deprecation and a
fondness for verbal trickery
and experimentation. He was
one of the early exponents of
vers libre and a major influence
on Pound and, particularly,
the young T.S. Eliot.

Poems
Anvil Press pbk £11.95

Poem by Mallarmé

Lorca, Federico Garcia
(1898 - 1936)

Lorca's fame and popularity as
a poet was established by
*Romancero Gitano (The Gypsy
Ballads)*, a striking collection
in which he revitalised a
traditional Spanish verse form
by the inclusion of modern
material and Freudian
symbolism and metaphors. In
the early thirties he became
more interested in the
possibilities of drama - plays
such as *Blood Wedding* and
Yerma date from these years -
but continued to write poetry,
perhaps most memorably
*Lament for the Death of a
Bullfighter,* a four-part poem
which addresses different
aspects of the goring and
death of a bullfighter who had
been a friend of Lorca. Lorca
himself was murdered by
Nationalists in the early days
of the Spanish Civil War.

Selected Poems
Bloodaxe pbk £8.95

Mallarmé, Stéphane
(1842 - 1898)

Mallarmé's earliest poetry was
influenced by the Romantics
and by Baudelaire but he
emerged from a spritual crisis
in 1866 intent upon what he
called his Grand Oeuvre, a
great work (never finished but
worked upon for the rest of
his life) which would embody
his notions of the ideal beauty
he saw as being the ultimate
reality, ultimately expressed in
poetry. Art was to be elevated
to the status of religion. In
search of this ideal and in
search of the 'musicality' of
poetry Mallarmé was led to
use elaborate symbols and
metaphors, to experiment
with rhythm and syntax and
with the arrangement of words
on the printed page. His work
is often obscure and
demanding but he had
enormous influence on
French poetry in the
generation after his death and
on modern European poetry
in general.

Selected Poems
University of California Press pbk £8.95

Mandelstam, Osip

(1891 - ?1938)

Together with Akhmatova and Gumilev, Mandelstam was one of the leading figures in the Acmeist Guild of poets and *Stone*, his first collection, was characterised by the precision and clarity that the guild members saw as essential to their poetic credo. After the revolution Mandelstam was long out of step with the new literary establishment, although he published further collections in 1922 and 1928. He was arrested in 1934 after reciting a poem denouncing Stalin and began the harrowing journey to his death, on his way to the labour camps, recorded movingly in his widow's memoirs *Hope Against Hope* and *Hope Abandoned*. The period between his two arrests, in 1934 and 1938, was also the period in which he wrote the important cycle of poetry known as the *Voronezh Notebooks*. The fact that his late poetry survived to bear a moral witness to the horrors of the Stalinist era is partly due to the heroic efforts of his wife who dedicated the rest of her life to his poetry, memorizing much of it in order to keep it alive during the times when its publication was impossible. Mandelstam is now considered to be one of the major poets of the century.

Selected Poems
Anvil Press pbk £5.95

Selected Poems
Penguin pbk £6.99

Voronezh Notebooks
Bloodaxe pbk £7.95

Michelangelo

(1475 - 1564)

The Renaissance sculptor and painter, creator of the gigantic marble statue of David in Florence and of the frescos on the ceiling of the Sistine chapel, was also the author of around three hundred sonnets which constitute a compelling spiritual autobiography.

Letters and Poetry
Oxford UP pbk £7.95

Sonnets
(trans. Elizabeth Jennings)
Carcanet pbk £6.95

Milosz, Czeslaw

(1911 -)

Milosz was born in Lithuania and studied law at the University of Vilnius, publishing his first book of poetry in his ealy twenties. He was a member of the Catastrophist group of poets, so-called because of their predictions of approaching catastrophe, a justifiable fear in the period. During the Nazi occupation Milosz was an active member of the Resistance and was responsible for much clandestine anti-Nazi publications. He fled to the West in the early fifties and became, eventually, a naturalised American citizen. In 1953 he published *The Captive Mind*, a famous denunciation of those intellectuals who acquiesced in the Communist system. His poetry presents a great variety of forms, ranging from mock odes and treatises in the spirit of the 18th century to notebooks of dreams. Joseph Brodsky has described Milosz as 'one of the greatest poets of our time, perhaps the greatest.'

Collected Poems
Penguin pbk £10.99

Montale, Eugenio
(1896 - 1981)

Generally acknowledged as the greatest of Italian poets this century, Montale won the Nobel Prize for Literature in 1975. His ability to draw on a wide range of language, from dialect to scientific terminology, the subtlety and sophistication of his wit and his interest in the suggestiveness and allusiveness of words all mark him out as a significant and rewarding writer.

The Coastguard's House
Bloodaxe pbk £7.95

Neruda, Pablo
(1904 - 1973)

Arguably the greatest, and certainly one of the most prolific of Latin American poets, the Chilean Pablo Neruda showed his precocious talent by publishing his first volume of poetry by the age of seventeen. He had developed his own poetic voice by his second volume, *Crepusculario,* and his third *Veinte poemas de amor y una cancion desesperada (Twenty love poems and a song of despair)* remains one of the most famous and admired books of erotic poetry this century. Increasing political influence led to Neruda travelling widely in ambassadorial roles and inevitably led his poetry away from the personal and towards a more grand scale, as seen in the *Residencias,* the last of which were influenced by his experience of the Spanish Civil War. The most ambitious of all of Neruda's works is the epic *Canto General* (1950), a series of fifteen cantos which is a history of Latin America, and contains the magnificent *Alturas de Macchu Picchu* (The Heights of Macchu Picchu), thought by many to be his finest single achievement. He was honoured with the Nobel Prize in 1968.

Canto General
University of California Press pbk £12.95

Selected Poems
Penguin pbk £7.99

Twenty Love Poems and a Song of Despair
Cape pbk £6.99

Boris Pasternak

Pasternak, Boris
(1890 - 1960)

Best known in the West for his novel *Dr Zhivago,* Pasternak was awarded the Nobel Prize for Literature in 1958 but obliged by the Soviet authorities to renounce it. In Russia his greatest renown is as a poet. He published his first collection before the revolution and further collections followed in the twenties but in 1933 he began what he described as his 'long, silent duel' with Stalin and the Soviet literary establishment. He was unable to publish original work for ten years and devoted his time to translation, including several highly regarded versions of Shakespeare plays. His chief commitment nonetheless remained to poetry and even his great novel is, in some sense, concerned with the creation of poetry. Indeed some of his finest verse, the culmination of his attempts to attain simplicity without sacrificing subtlety and complexity of expression, is that attributed to Zhivago in the novel.

Selected Poems
Penguin pbk £6.99

Paz, Octavio
(1914 -)

Paz is undoubtedly one of the major figures of Latin American letters this century, having managed, as have most of the successful writers of the continent, to transcend the historic regionalism that afflicted much of its literature. As with many major Latin American literary figures, Paz has spent much of his life abroad, including (again typically) a diplomatic career. Paz's prodigious output includes essays, translations, intellectual histories and criticism as well as poetry, although it is his poetry which has established his reputation. Starting from a fundamental belief in the corruption of Western values, he embarked on a long intellectual quest which embraced Marxism, Surrealism and ultimately Hinduism, an influence which is partly attributable to his having spent six years as Mexican ambassador to India. All of this can be traced in his poetry, which includes some landmark volumes, notably the prose poem *Aguila o sol? (Eagle or Sun?)* in 1951 and *Piedra de Sol (Sunstone)* in 1957.

Collected Poems 1957 - 1987
Carcanet pbk £6.95

Selected Poems
Penguin pbk £7.99

Pessoa, Fernando
(1888 - 1935)

Pessoa is now recognised as the most important Portuguese poet since Camoens and one of the outstanding figures in European modernism, although he published little in his lifetime. To encompass his many-sided poetic imagination he created three further personae - Alberto Caeiro, Ricardo Reis and Alvaro de Campos - who wrote poetry in three very different styles. Far more than merely pseudonyms, Caeiro, Reis and de Campos were the means of liberating Pessoa from the constraints of a unitary personality and release poetic qualities within himself otherwise unattainable.

Selected Poems
Penguin pbk £6.99

Petrarch
(1304 - 1374)

During his lifetime Petrarch was renowned as a scholar and student of classical culture but today he is remembered chiefly as the poet of a series of love poems addressed to an unidentified woman whom he calls Laura. His major influence on European culture has been the result of his development of the Petrarchan sonnet, a form which was later adapted into English to create the Shakespearean sonnet and also into all the other pricipal languages of the continent.

Lyric Poems
Harvard UP pbk £11.95

Selections from Canzoniere and other works
Oxford UP pbk £5.95

Pushkin, Alexander
(1799 - 1837)

Russia's greatest poet was born into an aristocratic family and worked in government service before being banished from St Petersburg for writing poems critical of the Tsar and his rule. A further exile, to his mother's estate, prevented Pushkin from compromising entanglement with the revolt in 1825 of the Decembrists, many of whom he knew and with whose aims he sympathised. He was allowed to return to Moscow the following year and continued to produce work prolifically in a variety of genres, including his most sophisticated achievement, the novel in verse *Eugene Onegin*. In 1837 he was fatally wounded in a duel. His influence on Russian literature has been felt by every major writer since.

Eugene Onegin
Penguin pbk £6.99

Rilke, Rainer Maria
(1875 - 1926)

Rilke is the most important German lyric poet of the century and has exerted a major influence on modern poetry. Always self-consciously aware of his calling as a poet, he developed from the subjectivity of his early verse, still in the grip of the spent force of late Romanticism, into a writer with a more concrete, objective grasp of the visual world. This is clear in *Neue Gedichte (New Poems)* of 1907-8, work much influenced by his experience of working as secretary to the French sculptor Rodin in Paris. The *Duino Elegies*, which he worked on throughout the First World War and beyond, can be seen, in their supple language, daring metrical experimentation and profound search for significance in what seemed a spiritually dead world, to be his greatest achievement. Finishing the cycle of Duino Elegies, Rilke went on to write, in a burst of almost manic creativity, the *Sonnets to Orpheus,* fifty five poems in which he endeavours to show art's power to transform and give meaning to the world.

Duino Elegies
Carcanet pbk £6.95

Selected Poems
Penguin pbk £5.95

Unofficial Rilke
Anvil Press pbk £6.95

Rimbaud, Arthur
(1854 - 1891)

Rimbaud's life is an extraordinary story of precocity and repudiation of remarkable gifts. His fierce independence of all forms of orthodoxy was fully in place by his mid-teens and in 1871 he wrote the first of his major poems *Le Bateau Ivre.* This brought him to the attention of Paul Verlaine with whom he conducted an intense and violent relationship over the next two years, ending when Verlaine shot and wounded him, resulting in the older man's arrest and imprisonment. This was also the period in which Rimbaud wrote his two collections of prose poems, *Illuminations* and *Un Saison en Enfer,* and developed most fully his theory of the poet as seer who, through a conscious 'dereglement des sens', should break down conventional concepts of the personality in order to express the otherwise

inexpressible. From 1875 Rimbaud abandoned literature and led a nomadic life, first in Europe, then in North Africa where he became a trader in, among other goods, guns and arms. As a poet Rimbaud was strongly influenced by Baudelaire but he went further than any previous poet in the exploration of the irrational depths of the mind and in experimentation with the use of words solely for their evocative and sensational qualities. His influence on modern French poetry has been profound.

Collected Poems
Penguin pbk £8.99

Complete Works
University of Chicago Press pbk £11.25

Season in Hell & Other Poems
Anvil Press pbk £7.95

Seferis, George
(1900 - 1971)

Born in Smyrna, Seferis became a diplomat and spent several years in Britain where he was Greek ambassador from 1957 to 1962. He won the Nobel Prize for Literature in 1963. His exacting Apollonian poetry is characterised by a remarkable imagistic vision and concise, allusive language ; it is steeped in the myths and literature of the classical Greek past.

Complete Poems
Anvil Press pbk £9.95

Strassburg, Gottfried von
(FL. 1210)

No information is extant about Gottfried's life beyond the little that can be gleaned from his own work and references to him by other poets. The writer of the unfinished *Tristan und Isolde,* the most authoritative of the medieval versions of the legend, was clearly a man of some learning accustomed to the life of the courts at which his epic would have been recited.

Tristan
Penguin pbk £6.99

Tagore, Rabindranath
(1861 - 1941)

Tagore was a man of wide talents and wrote novels and short stories as well as poetry in his native Bengali. He was also a painter and composer, setting many of his poems to music. He won the Nobel Prize for Literature in 1913, the first Asian writer to do so, largely on the strength of his best known collection *Gitanjali,* which had been originally published in India three years previously and then translated by Tagore himself into English prose poems. In his poetic work Tagore creates an impressive fusion of East and West, importing Western verse forms into Bengali literature, and of tradition with restless innovation. Most of all he creates a poetry of compassion and humanity which transcends cultural barriers.

I Won't Let You Go: Selected Poems
Bloodaxe pbk £9.95

Selected Poems
Penguin pbk £7.99

Troyes, Chretien de
(FL.1170 -1190)

A French poet who wrote five Arthurian romances in the second half of the 12th century, skilfully combining narrative art with the development of the notion of courtly love. All are written in octosyllabic rhyming couplets and provide versions of such familiar stories as those of Percival and the search for the Holy Grail and of Sir Lancelot. His influence on all subsequent Arthurian literature is immense.

Arthurian Romances
Penguin pbk £8.99

Arthurian Romances
Dent pbk £6.99

Tsvetayeva, Marina
(1892 - 1941)

Unlike many of the major poets of her generation in Russia, Tsvetayeva responded with hostility to the Revolution of 1917. Her husband fought in the White Army against the Bolsheviks and, after the latter's eventual victory in the civil war, they went into exile, an exile that dominated her life and much of her poetry. She lived for much of the twenties and thirties in great poverty in Paris, producing verse which reflected growing disillusionment with emigré life and a profound nostalgia for her motherland. She returned to Russia in 1939 but, two years later, she was evacuated from Moscow to a remote provincial town where she committed suicide. Her work has been rediscovered and reassessed in the last thirty years, both in Russia and in the West, and has been much admired for its innovative use of language and rhythm.

Selected Poems
Bloodaxe pbk £7.95

Selected Poems
Oxford UP pbk £9.99

Valéry, Paul
(1871 - 1945)

Valéry's poetic career is curiously divided. In his twenties, deeply influenced by Mallarmé and the Symbolists, he wrote and published a small number of poems. He then abandoned poetry for fifteen years, only returning to it when he was prevailed upon to collect his earlier verse and write a new introductory poem. This took him four years and became eventually *La Jeune Parque*, a famously demanding long poem which has been recently made available in a newly clarifying translation. His other major collection, *Charmes*, published in 1922, includes *Le Cimetière Marin*, a meditation on death, its inevitability and its acceptance, which is set in the cemetery at Sete where Valéry himself now lies buried.

La Jeune Parque
Bloodaxe pbk £6.95

Vallejo, Cesar
(1892 - 1938)

The Peruvian Cesar Vallejo is widely regarded as one of the pivotal figures in the genesis of contemporary Latin American literature. His first work, *Los Heraldos Negros (The Black Heralds)*, written in 1918, was followed by the untranslatable neologism *Trilce* (1922), which was to stand as his most important volume, and which contains some of the most highly charged and syntactically ambitious poetry ever written in Spanish. It was also one of the first works in Latin America to have an authentically regional voice, without looking to Europe for influence.

Selected Poetry
F Cairns pbk £6.95

Verlaine, Paul
(1844 - 1896)

The sensational trajectory of
Verlaine's difficult life - his
doubly besotted relationship
with Rimbaud, his spells in
prison and his alternating
spells of reckless intoxication
and fierce repentance and
remorse - is only too likely to
obscure the achievements of
his verse. The poetry he wrote
while he wandered Europe,
drunkenly quarrelling with
Rimbaud, published in 1874 as
Romances sans Paroles,
influenced the emerging
Symbolist movement and his
collection ten years later *Jadis
et naguère,* with its emphasis on
the fluidity and musicality of
verse and the necessity to
escape the rigid straitjackets of
rhyme and regular metre, was
equally important. He also
wrote religious lyrics inspired
by his characteristically
changeable relationship with
the Catholic church as well as
much erotic verse.

Women/Men
Anvil Press pbk £8.95

Selected Poems
University of California Press pbk £10.95

Villon, Francois
(1431 - AFTER 1463)

The little information that
exists about France's greatest
medieval poet suggests a life
spent in almost constant
uproar and violence.
Banished from Paris for the
killing of a priest, Villon
suffered a series of
incarcerations, was
sentenced to death in the
aftermath of another brawl -
a sentence that was
commuted to further
banishment - and disappears
from the records in 1463.
His range of poetic voices
from (literally) gallows
humour to lyric expression
of love, compassion for his
fellow man and regret for
the mistakes of the past is
remarkable in an oeuvre of
only about 3,000 surviving
lines.

Selected Poems
Penguin pbk £6.99

Yevtushenko, Yevgeny
(1933 -)

Since his early twenties
Yevtushenko has been seen as
the representative poet of the
first post-Stalin generation and
his work has been enormously
popular in Russia where his
readings have filled clubs,
factory halls and even sports
stadiums. He echoes the early
poets of the Revolution, poets
like Mayakovsky and Esenin,
in his use of colloquial
language and the reworking
of lyric forms. After the
publication of *Babi Yar,* written
after a visit to the site of a Nazi
massacre of Ukrainian Jews,
he travelled and gave readings
in the West, although there
was some official discomfort
with a work that suggested a
lingering anti-semitism in
Russian society. His *Collected
Poems* appeared in 1990.

Collected Poems 1952-1990
Mainstream hbk £20.00

Poetry Anthologies

There are many hundreds of poetry anthologies in print. The following is a small selection of the most engaging, stimulating and wide-ranging.

After Ovid: New Metamorphoses
Edited by Michael Hoffmann and James Lasdun

This collection of contemporary 'translations' of the work of the Roman poet Ovid by 42 different modern poets throws up a remarkable variety of styles and solutions to the challenge of his work. Poets as different as Hughes, Heaney, Shapcott and Les Murray have contributed, and the result works as a guide both to the contemporary poetry scene and to Ovid himself.

Faber and Faber pbk £8.99

The Penguin Book of American Verse
Edited by Geoffrey Moore

First published in 1977, Geoffrey Moore's collection covers the whole American poetic tradition from the seventeenth to the twentieth century, while paying particular attention to the explosion of creativity that followed the 1950s.

Penguin pbk £8.99

A Choice of Anglo-Saxon Verse
Selected by Richard Hamer

A selection of all the most famous short poems of Old English. Each is published in its original version, and Richard Hamer provides the reader with a parallel verse translation as well as an informed introduction.

Faber and Faber pbk £7.99

The Oxford Book of Comic Verse
Edited by John Gross

From Chaucer and Shakespeare to E.J. Thribb and Victoria Wood, this delightful collection of humorous verse scours the centuries in search of poetry that will amuse and entertain.

Oxford University Press pbk £7.99

The Penguin Book of Contemporary British Poetry
Edited by Blake Morrison and Andrew Motion

Published in 1982, this landmark anthology introduced and championed a whole generation of now familiar names – among them Craig Raine, Tony Harrison, James Fenton, Fleur Adcock and Morrison and Motion themselves – and confirmed the emergence of a new spirit and a new confidence in British poetry.

Penguin pbk £6.99

The Earliest English Poems
Translated and Introduced by Michael Alexander

Anglo-Saxon poetry between 700 and 1000 paid particular attention to technical accomplishment, and for this anthology Michael Alexander has translated the best Old English poetry into a verse form that retains the qualities of Anglo-Saxon metre and alliteration.

Penguin pbk £6.99

The New Oxford Book of Eighteenth Century Verse
Edited by Roger Lonsdale

As well as the familiar tradition of Pope, Swift and Blake, this comprehensive anthology also includes the work of many forgotten eighteenth-century writers from all levels of society. Full of life and humour, the book has done much to redefine the period's poetic sensibilities.

Oxford University Press pbk £11.99

Emergency Kit
Edited by Jo Shapcott and Matthew Sweeney

Subtitled 'Poetry from Strange Times', this important new anthology of contemporary English-language poetry from across the world ventures beyond Britain, Ireland and the United States to take in the whole of the English-speaking world. Refreshing in its approach and exuberant in its choice, the book takes delight in upsetting convention and attacking prejudice.

Faber and Faber pbk £9.99

The New Oxford Book of English Verse
Edited by Helen Gardner

Reaching back as far as 1250 and weighing in at 800 pages, Dame Helen Gardner's 1972 anthology is certainly all-encompassing in its embrace. The sheer quantity of poems·included means that there is ample room for pleasant surprises alongside the more familiar verse.

Oxford University Press hbk £19.99

The Oxford Book of English Verse 1250-1918
Edited by Sir Arthur Quiller-Couch

Alongside Palgrave's Golden Treasury, this first and most famous Oxford anthology of verse – published originally in 1900, with a second edition following in 1939 – has established itself as the classic collection of English poetry.

Oxford University Press hbk £17.99

The Penguin Book of English Verse
Edited by John Hayward

Verse in English rather than verse by English people is the subject of this 1956 anthology, which includes everyone from Emily Dickinson to Dylan Thomas in a collection that spans four and a half centuries from 1500 to the 1950s.

Penguin pbk £5.99

The Oxford Book of Twentieth Century English Verse
Chosen by Philip Larkin

This celebrated anthology of modern English verse – which was conceived originally as a successor to W.B. Yeats' Oxford Book of Modern Verse 1892-1935 – is fascinating not just for the quality of its individual entries but also for what it tells us about the tastes of Larkin himself.

Oxford University Press hbk £17.99.

The Penguin Book of German Verse
Introduced and edited by Leonard Forster.

First published in 1957, Leonard Forster's long-serving anthology is a useful introduction for English readers to the German poetic tradition. Each poem is accompanied by a plain prose translation, and the book covers every significant movement from medieval lyrics and Protestant hymns, through Goethe and Schiller to expressionism and beyond.

Penguin pbk £8.99

The Penguin Book of Greek Verse
Introduced and Edited by Constantine A. Trypanis

'Poetry written in Greek constitutes the longest uninterrupted tradition in the Western World.' So writes Professor Trypanis in his introduction to this anthology, which offers plain prose translations of the finest examples of Greek poetry from the last three thousand years.

Penguin pbk £13.00

Hinterland: Caribbean Poetry from the West Indies and Britain
Edited by E.A. Markham

This essential primer on Caribbean Poetry contains substantial selections from the work of fourteen poets – including Derek Walcott, Grace Nichols and Linton Kwesi Johnson – as well as interviews and essays by the poets on their work.

Bloodaxe pbk £9.95

The Faber Book of Irish Verse
Edited by John Montague

Eclectic in its choices and sound in its judgments, John Montague's 1974 anthology of Irish poetry is a delightful introduction to the riches of the Irish poetic tradition.

Faber and Faber pbk £11.99

The New Oxford Book of Irish Verse
Edited by Thomas Kinsella

This ground-breaking anthology was the first comprehensive attempt to present the entire range of Irish poetry – in both Gaelic and English – for an English-speaking readership. Moving from the earliest, pre-Christian times through Swift and Goldsmith to Yeats and his successors, the book successfully presents the Irish tradition as a unity.

Oxford University Press pbk £9.99

The Faber Book of Love Poems
Edited by Geoffrey Grigson

Grigson, one of the century's great poetry anthologists, had no truck with the idea that most love poems are just intellectual conceits or a verbal training ground for their authors. This rich and revealing collection, first published in 1977, includes all the expected gems - by Donne, Shakespeare et al - plus quite a few surprises.

Faber and Faber pbk £9.99

Medieval English Lyrics 1200-1400
Edited by Thomas G. Duncan

This selection of medieval verse covers an enormous range of moods and subjects, from devotional and love lyrics to penitential lyrics, satires and drinking songs. All have been made accessible for the contemporary reader and are supported by a thorough glossary and a full textual commentary.

Penguin pbk £7.99

The New Poetry
Edited by Michael Hulse, David Kennedy and David Morley

This anthology is over three years old now, but as an overview of the new generation of British and Irish poets that has grown up since the publication of Blake Morrison and Andrew Motion's Penguin Book of Contemporary British Poetry it remains unchallenged. Full of energy, ambition and drive, the 50 diverse and disparate voices collected here range from Paul Durcan and Carol Ann Duffy to Liz Lockhead and Fred D'Aguiar.

Bloodaxe pbk £8.95

Other Men's Flowers
Selected by Lord Wavell

As well as being a British army general, Lord Wavell was also a lifelong devotee of poetry. First published in 1944 at the height of the Second World War, this personal selection of his favourite verse is remarkable for its intensity, passion and honesty.

Pimlico pbk £10.00

Palgrave's Golden Treasury

Palgrave's Golden Treasury is the first port of call for anyone wanting to introduce themselves to the riches of British and Irish poetry. This classic anthology, first published in 1861, contains all the most famous poems in the canon, and the new sixth edition includes work by over 90 poets from the post-war period.

Oxford University Press pbk £8.99

Poetry with an Edge
Edited by Neil Astley

This anthology of verse by nearly eighty poets from Britain, Ireland, America, Europe and the Commonwealth was originally published to mark fifteen years of publishing by Bloodaxe Books and the vigorous and catholic choice reflects the qualities of a list which has been of central importance in British poetry during that period.

Bloodaxe pbk £8.95

The Rattle Bag
Edited by Ted Hughes and Seamus Heaney

Since it was first published in 1982 this superb anthology of verse has become the most popular introduction to the pleasures of poetry available. Hughes and Heaney say that their aim in compiling The Rattle Bag was 'to amplify notions of what poetry is' and a choice which ranges from Shakespeare to the prayers and incantations of tribal hunters certainly achieves that aim.

Faber & Faber pbk £9.99

English Romantic Verse
Edited by David Wright

As well as collecting together all the most striking and important poems by the major Romantics – Blake, Wordsworth, Coleridge, Byron, Shelley, Clare and Keats – this excellent anthology also includes work by their eighteenth-century precursors and by their successors, poets such as Beddoes and Poe.

Penguin pbk £7.99

Poetry of the Thirties
Edited by Robin Skelton

A powerful and illuminating anthology which arranges the poetry of Auden, Day Lewis, Spender, MacNeice and the other key poets of the thirties into a 'critical essay' of this troubled and creative decade.

Penguin pbk £6.99

The New Oxford Book of Victorian Verse
Edited by Christopher Ricks

Victorian poetry found a champion in this exhaustive collection, whose coverage of every type of work – Emily Brontë as well as Tennyson, nonsense verse as well as Hopkins – does full justice to the age and its artists.

Oxford University Press pbk £10.99

The Faber Book of War Poetry
Edited by Kenneth Baker

Tory politician Kenneth Baker is a gifted anthologist and, in this new volume, he turns his attention to his most demanding subject so far – the poetry of war. The result is an enormously wide-ranging collection of work by poets as diverse as Heine and Wilfred Owen, Dylan Thomas and Stephen Crane, divided into sections dealing with every aspect of warfare from 'Gallantry and Heroism' to 'The Consolations of Obscenity.'

Faber and Faber hbk £17.50

The Oxford Book of War Poetry
Edited by Jon Stallworthy

This powerful collection ranges across the whole history of warfare. Arranged chronologically by conflict, the book moves from the Bible and Homer, through the explosion of poetry associated with the two world wars, to verse written in response to more recent conflicts.

Oxford University Press pbk £7.99

The Faber Book of 20th Century Women's Poetry
Edited by Fleur Adcock

An anthology of twentieth-century Women's Poetry that is comprehensive in its coverage and catholic in its tastes. Covering everyone from Marianne Moore and Sylvia Townsend Warner to Wendy Cope and Selima Hill, the book demonstrates the richness and variety of women's contributions to this century's literature.

Faber and Faber pbk £10.99

Sixty Women Poets
Edited by Linda France

An anthology which traces the extraordinary flowering of women's poetry in the two and a half decades since the death of Stevie Smith. As well as exploring the full range of modern voices, France – who is keen to emphasise the links that bind the new generation to the past – also includes work by poets like E.J. Scovell and Elizabeth Jennings.

Bloodaxe pbk £8.95

The Bloodaxe Book of Contemporary Women's Verse
Edited by Jeni Couzyn

Too often anthologies do scant justice to the poets represented because they present so little of their work. This popular anthology concentrates on eleven poets only – they include Sylvia Plath, Fleur Adcock, Jenny Joseph and Elizabeth Jennings – and provides a generous selection of their work, together with illuminating introductory essays.

Bloodaxe pbk £9.95

Services at Waterstone's

Recommendation

Our booksellers really know and care about what they are selling. If you need help, please don't hesitate to ask.

Writers at Waterstone's

Ask at your branch for details of author events (including poetry events).

Waterstone's Mailing Service

If you wish to order your books by post, please contact: Waterstone's Mailing Service, 4-5 Milsom Street, Bath BA1 1DA

Booksearch

Waterstone's Booksearch service will try to track down out-of-print books for you. Booksearch, 32-40 Calverley Road, Tunbridge Wells, TN1 2TD

Signed First Editions

A choice of up to 150 of the year's finest fiction and non-fiction titles – all signed by the author and posted to you. Waterstone's Signed First Editions Collection, 4-5 Milsom Street, Bath BA1 1DA

Waterstone's Book Vouchers

Accepted in over 500 bookshops in the United Kingdom and Ireland, including all branches of WH Smith.

For information about any Waterstone's service, please ask a bookseller.

£1 off

any Everyman's Library Pocket Poets

Cut out this coupon, fill in your name and address on the reverse
and we shall happily give you £1 off any
title in the Everyman Pocket Poets Library.

This coupon is worth £1 off a single purchase of any title in the Everyman Pocket Poets Library.
It is valid until 31st May 1997 and may not be transferred for cash.
The information overleaf is covered and bound by the terms and conditions of the Data Protection Act and will be used only in connection with
products and services provided by Waterstone's.

....

£1 off

any Faber poetry title

Cut out this coupon, fill in your name and address on the reverse
and we shall happily give you £1 off any
Faber poetry book.

This coupon is worth £1 off a single purchase of any Faber poetry title. It is valid until 31st May 1997 and may not be transferred for cash.
The information overleaf is covered and bound by the terms and conditions of the Data Protection Act and will be used only in connection with
products and services provided by Waterstone's.

....

£1 off

any Carcanet poetry title

Cut out this coupon, fill in your name and address on the reverse
and we shall happily give you £1 off any
Carcanet poetry book.

This coupon is worth £1 off a single purchase of any Carcanet poetry title. It is valid until 31st May 1997 and may not be transferred for cash.
The information overleaf is covered and bound by the terms and conditions of the Data Protection Act and will be used only in connection with
products and services provided by Waterstone's.

Name...

Address...

....

....

....

....Postcode.........................

Please tick this box if you do not wish to receive further information about Waterstone's ☐

For booksellers users only:

Branch ....Till Receipt no...............................Amount spend........................

Name...

Address...

....

....

....

....Postcode.........................

Please tick this box if you do not wish to receive further information about Waterstone's ☐

For booksellers users only:

Branch ....Till Receipt no...............................Amount spend........................

Name...

Address...

....

....

....

....Postcode.........................

Please tick this box if you do not wish to receive further information about Waterstone's ☐

For booksellers users only:

Branch ....Till Receipt no...............................Amount spend........................

IN THE TRADITION OF
THE GREAT PRIVATE PRESS BOOKS OF
THE TWENTIES AND THIRTIES, THE EVERYMAN'S
POCKET POETS LIBRARY IS A SERIES OF TWENTY FOUR
BEAUTIFULLY PRODUCED TITLES, ALL PRINTED, BOUND AND DESIGNED
TO CREATE THE STANDARD AND QUALITY THAT GREAT POETRY DESERVES. THE TITLES IN PRINT ARE:

Charles Baudelaire, William Blake, Emily Bronte, Samuel Taylor Coleridge, Emily Dickinson, John Donne, Gerard Manley Hopkins, John Keats, John Milton, Edgar Allan Poe, Rainer Maria Rilke, Arthur Rimbaud, Christina Rossetti, William Shakespeare, Percy Shelley, Walt Whitman, William Wordsworth, W.B. Yeats, Animal Poems, Erotic Poems, Poems of Friendship, Love Poems, Garden Poems , Love Letters

'What lovely, lovely little books these are.'
JOHN UPDIKE

Index

Where to find your nearest Waterstone's

ABERDEEN
236 Union Street
Tel: 01224 571655

BATH
4–5 Milsom Street
Tel: 01225 448515

University of Bath
Claverton Down
Tel: 01225 465565

BELFAST
Queen's Building
8 Royal Avenue
Tel: 01232 247355

BIRMINGHAM
24–26 High Street
Tel: 0121 633 4353
Fax: 0121 633 4300
Young Waterstone's
Tel: 0121 616 1557

BOURNEMOUTH
14/16 The Arcade
Tel: 01202 299449

BRADFORD
The Wool Exchange
(opening October 1996)

University of Bradford,
Great Horton Road
Tel: 01274 727885

Management Centre Bookshop,
Emm Lane
Tel: 01274 481404

BRIGHTON
55–56 North Street
Tel: 01273 327867

BRISTOL
27–29 College Green
Tel: 0117 925 0511

Computer Centre
University of Bristol
Tyndall Avenue
Tel: 0117 925 4297

The Galleries
Broadmead
Tel: 0117 925 2274
Fax: 0117 925 9275

BROMLEY
20-22 Market Square
Tel: 0181 464 6562

CAMBRIDGE
6 Bridge Street
Tel: 01223 300123
Fax: 01223 301539

CANTERBURY
20 St Margarets St
Tel: 01227 456343

CARDIFF
2a The Hayes
Tel: 01222 665606

CHELTENHAM
88–90 The Promenade
Tel: 01242 512722

CHESTER
43–45 Bridge Street Row
Tel: 01244 328040

COLCHESTER
The Old Library
16 Culver Precinct
Tel: 01206 767623

University of Essex
Wivenhoe Park
Tel: 01206 864773

CORK
69 Patrick Street
Tel: 00 353 21 276522

Boole Library Basement,
University College
Tel: 00 353 21 276575

CROYDON
1063 Whitgift Centre
Tel: 0181 686 7032

DERBY
78-80 St Peter's Street
Tel: 01332 296997

DORKING
54–60 South Street
Tel: 01306 886884

DUBLIN
7 Dawson Street
Tel: 00 353 16 791260

Jervis Centre
(opening November 1996)

DUNDEE
35 Commercial Street,
Tel: 01382 200322

DURHAM
69 Saddler Street
Tel: 0191 383 1488

EASTBOURNE
120 Terminus Road
Tel: 01323 735676

EDINBURGH
128 Princes Street
Tel: 0131 226 2666

13–14 Princes Street
Tel: 0131 556 3034/5

83 George Street
Tel: 0131 225 3436

EPSOM
113 High Street
Tel: 01372 741713

EXETER
48–49 High Street
Tel: 01392 218392

GATESHEAD
17 The Parade
Metro Centre
Tel: 0191 493 2715

GATWICK
North Terminal
Airside
Gatwick Airport
Tel: 01293 507112

GLASGOW
132 Union Street
Tel: 0141 221 0890

45–50 Princes Square
Tel: 0141 221 9650

GUILDFORD
35–39 North Street
Tel: 01483 302919

HANLEY, STOKE-ON-TRENT
The Tontines Centre
Parliament Row
Tel: 01782 204582

HULL
University of Hull
University House
Tel: 01482 444190

The Grand Buildings,
Jameson Street
Tel: 01482 580234

IPSWICH
15 -19 Buttermarket
Tel: 01473 289044

KINGSTON-UPON-THAMES
23–25 Thames Street
Tel: 0181 547 1221

LANCASTER
2–8 King Street
Tel: 01524 61477

LEAMINGTON SPA
Unit 1, Priorsgate
Warwick Street
Tel: 01926 883804

LEEDS
36–38 Albion Street
Tel: 0113 242 0839

93–97 Albion Street
Tel: 0113 244 4588

LEICESTER
The Shires
21/23 High Street
Tel: 0116 251 6838

LIVERPOOL
52 Bold Street
Tel: 0151 709 0866

LONDON

CAMDEN
128 Camden High Street NW1
Tel: 0171 284 4948

CHARING CROSS ROAD
121 Charing Cross Road WC2
Tel: 0171 434 4291

THE CITY
1 Whittington Ave
Leadenhall Market EC3
Tel: 0171 220 7882

COVENT GARDEN
9 Garrick Street WC2
Tel: 0171 836 6757

EARL'S COURT
266 Earl's Court Road SW5
Tel: 0171 370 1616

GOLDSMITH'S
Goldsmith's College
New Cross SE14
Tel: 0181 469 0262

HAMPSTEAD
68 Hampstead High Street NW3
Tel: 0171 794 1098

HARRODS
87 Brompton Road SW1
Tel: 0171 730 1234
Fax: 0171 225 5920

ISLINGTON
10-12 Islington Green, N1
Tel: 0171 704 2280

KENSINGTON
193 Kensington High Street W8
Tel: 0171 937 8432

NOTTING HILL
39 Notting Hill Gate W11
Tel: 0171 229 9444

OLD BROMPTON ROAD
99 Old Brompton Road SW7
Tel: 0171 581 8522

WIMBLEDON
12 Wimbledon Bridge SW19
Tel: 0181 543 9899

MAIDSTONE
19 Earl Street
Tel: 01622 681112

MAILING SERVICE
(see Bath Milsom St)
Tel: 01225 448595
Fax: 01225 444732

MANCHESTER
91 Deansgate
Tel: 0161 832 1992

MIDDLESBROUGH
9 Newton Mall
Cleveland Centre
Tel: 01642 242682

Teesside
University Bookshop
1 King Edward Square
Tel: 01642 242017

NEWCASTLE
104 Grey Street
Tel: 0191 261 6140

NORTHAMPTON
19 Abington Street
Tel: 01604 34854

NORWICH
Royal Arcade
Tel: 01603 632426

University of East Anglia,
University Plain
Tel: 01603 453625

NOTTINGHAM
1–5 Bridlesmith Gate
Tel: 0115 9484499

PERTH
St John's Centre
Tel: 01738 630013

PETERBOROUGH
6 Queensgate
Tel: 01733 313476

PLYMOUTH
65/69 New George Street
Tel: 01752 256699

PRESTON
3–5 Fishergate
Tel: 01772 555766

READING
89a Broad Street
Tel: 01722 581270

RICHMOND-UPON-THAMES
2–6 Hill Street
Tel: 0181 332 1600

SALISBURY
7/9 High Street
Tel: 01722 415596

SHEFFIELD
24 Orchard Square
Tel: 0114 2728971

SHREWSBURY
18–19 High Street
Tel: 01743 248112

SOUTHAMPTON
69 Above Bar
Tel: 01703 633130

Southampton Medical School,
South Academic Block,
Southampton General Hospital
Tel: 01703 780602

University of Southampton,
Highfield
Tel: 01703 558267

SOUTHEND-ON-SEA
49-55 High Street
Tel: 01702 437480

SOUTHPORT
367 Lord Street
Tel: 01704 501088

STOCKPORT
103 Princes Street
Tel: 0161 477 3755

STRATFORD-UPON-AVON
18 The High Street
Tel: 01789 414418

SWANSEA
The Old Carlton Cinema,
Oxford Street
Tel: 01792 463567

SWINDON
27 Regent Street
Tel: 01793 488838

TUNBRIDGE WELLS
32/40 Calverley Road
Tel: 01892 535446

WATFORD
174-176 The Harlequin Centre,
High Street
Tel: 01923 218197

WINCHESTER
1/2 Kings Walk
Tel: 01962 866206

WORCESTER
95 High Street
Tel: 01905 723397

YORK
28–29 High Ousegate
Tel: 01904 628740